AF839392

Being at Work

This thought-provoking and ground-breaking book offers a way for us all to consider our experience of being at work, and of the nature of working life. Written in an engaging and accessible style, it presents the practical means by which to apply central features of existentialism to make sense of how we relate to work and the workplace.

These include topics such as freedom and choice, looking for purpose and making meaning, and authenticity. We spend a great deal of time at work, and being at work is often a challenge. Reference to the past in a corporate context tends to see it as a graveyard for errors and failures; the future is something articulated by senior leaders and the place to which we are expected to travel, in terms of their definition. The (specious) present is the place where we experience our being in the moment, the location where we do our work … but it is rarely acknowledged in the places where we work. This book offers new insights into how we can all meaningfully live our lives in the context of the world of work. To do this, it offers a personalised understanding of the existentialist way of philosophising. It looks to simplify complex concepts in order to offer the reader a different way of thinking about the time that they spend at work and how they might consider different and more positive ways of being in such an environment. It recognises that we spend a considerable amount of our life in the workplace – and so argues that we need to consider that and find ways in which to make that experience personally meaningful.

Where other practices designed to help people to make sense of their actual experience are introspective, existentialism is reflexive and active. Similarly, where those other approaches are deeply individualistic, existentialism constantly reminds us that our choices are undertaken in relation to others … and that they have a collective implication. Whether you are keen to make sense of your experience of workplace – and what it means to be a human being in that context – or looking to explore how you embrace the challenges of being a leader in business, this book will offer you rich perspectives for sense making and ways of rethinking your presence at work.

Mark Cole has worked in a variety of developmental roles in organisations for nearly 40 years. He is the managing director of Radical OD Ltd, where he supports people to come together in dialogue to find different ways of being and doing in organisations.

Being at Work

Using Existentialism to Make Sense of Your Organisational Life

MARK COLE

Routledge
Taylor & Francis Group
LONDON AND NEW YORK

Designed cover image: Getty Images - alashi

First published 2026
by Routledge
4 Park Square, Milton Park, Abingdon, Oxon OX14 4RN

and by Routledge
605 Third Avenue, New York, NY 10158

Routledge is an imprint of the Taylor & Francis Group, an informa business

© 2026 Mark Cole

The right of Mark Cole to be identified as author of this work has been asserted in accordance with sections 77 and 78 of the Copyright, Designs and Patents Act 1988.

All rights reserved. No part of this book may be reprinted or reproduced or utilised in any form or by any electronic, mechanical, or other means, now known or hereafter invented, including photocopying and recording, or in any information storage or retrieval system, without permission in writing from the publishers.

Trademark notice: Product or corporate names may be trademarks or registered trademarks, and are used only for identification and explanation without intent to infringe.

British Library Cataloguing-in-Publication Data
A catalogue record for this book is available from the British Library

ISBN: 978-1-032-97186-5 (hbk)
ISBN: 978-1-032-95389-2 (pbk)
ISBN: 978-1-003-59262-4 (ebk)

DOI: 10.4324/9781003592624

Typeset in Dante and Avenir
by codeMantra

Contents

Acknowledgements

As ever, I want to thank my wife Sarah and son Thomas for all the support that they offer me in terms of my work and my writing. Their positivity about what I do is invaluable in terms of giving me the confidence and commitment to undertake a project like this. I hope that they both feel as supported by me as I do by them.

I want to publicly acknowledge the importance of my relationship with John Higgins. Our weekly hour-long conversations invariably leave me full of fresh insights and new ideas. And on this occasion John has been fantastic in terms of editing the drafts that I produced as I went through the process of writing. He is a truly talented writer and a brilliant thinker – and I count myself lucky to be able to have him as a colleague and a friend. Whilst I accepted many of John's extremely helpful suggestions and amendments, the responsibility for the final item lies of course exclusively with me.

I also want to mention Malcolm Freeman, the existential psychotherapist with whom I have been working over the past few years in order to attend to the anxiety that beset me with the arrival of the Covid pandemic. Not only have our weekly sessions helped me therapeutically, but they also reconnected me with existentialism and allowed me to think in depth about all of the various aspects of this philosophy.

My late parents also deserve mention, as I feel their positive influence every time I embark on a new piece of work or a fresh piece of writing. I am sad that both of them passed before my first book appeared, as I would have felt hugely proud to share that achievement with them.

There have been a number of people who have influenced me in terms of helping me reach a point where writing a book no longer felt like something people other than me would do. I am indebted to Neil Hall at the University of Greenwich, who – following an interview - offered me a place on the professional doctorate programme in the School of Education despite the fact that I had not completed a Masters. And I gained a huge amount from having Heather Brunskell-Evans as the supervisor of my doctoral thesis, in terms of productive challenge and rich insight.

Preface

A personal approach

In this book, I have attempted to weave together my intimate personal experiences with a rich understanding and application of key concepts arising out of existentialism as a way of philosophically engaging with the world. A good many of the instances to which I refer herein arose out of my reaction to the Covid-19 pandemic. From a clinical perspective, this was viewed as an acute anxiety disorder. On reflection, my existentialist understanding of anxiety as an intrinsic response to the actuality of being a human being has felt to me to be a better way of engaging now with how I felt.

In terms of making that adjustment, I have been very fortunate to have worked over the past few years with an existential psychotherapist. Our sessions have been helpfully therapeutic in a range of ways, but they have also offered me space for intellectual development, in terms of thinking about my place in the world and how I might thoughtfully navigate the living of my life.

Because of this, a lot of the material in this book starts with a description of an experience. Having sketched that out, I move on to make observations about having been immersed in these situations. Crucially, I then move on to reflect on the situation and my place and role within it, before offering my invariably altered thinking about these circumstances.

Hence, the first chapter offers an extensive autobiographical exploration of existentialism and its relevance based on my existence in the world – and in particular in light of my existence within the world of work. This is the focus of this work; it is an exposition on how we live our lives in the workplace, in light of the amount of time we spend in that environment. It also uses existentialist notions to actively challenge how we think about work and the structures within which we end up doing it. It envisages a radically different array of ways in which we can live our lives at work. It is not a manifesto: rather, it is a way of seeing the world differently and potentially shifting and changing our presence in that space to enhance our lives.

A philosophical understanding

Hence, Chapters 2–6 offer a careful consideration of life, particularly as lived in the workplace … and viewed through a range of key concepts that constitute existentialist philosophising with a focus on our individual existence, mindful of the roles ascribed to us in that context. There are explorations of themes such as: *freedom*; the experience of *temporality*, encompassing both our existential finitude and the way in which time is presented in the world of work; the creation of *meaning and purpose* in our respective lives and how that plays out in the realm of paid employment; the complex but essential issue of *choice* in human lives; and an exploration of the contrast between the corporate and the existential interpretations of *authenticity*.

Finally, in Chapter 7, I offer a practical drawing together of the corporate lessons that can be derived from the preceding analyses, so that everyone – whether manager or employee, leader or follower – can consider how to live their lives consistently with the crucial precepts of existentialism.

Negotiating the thinking and ideas

As ever with a work such as this, I have greatly enjoyed immersing myself in the thinking and writing that undergirds the philosophy. In terms of my own sense-making in respect of my experience of anxiety since 2020, I have accessed as wide a range of materials as possible – and have taken time to get deeply into that work. In most instances, this has been a delicious combination of joy and understanding. However, in the spirit of full disclosure, I am taking this opportunity to admit that despite my best efforts early on in the project, I found (and continue to find) the work of Heidegger utterly impenetrable. Early on, I endeavoured to read *Being and Time* but could not make any headway with it.

All of which means that references to Heidegger herein tend to be drawn from secondary sources, either in terms of direct quotations from those commentators or through those writers directing me to a specific observation that I was then able to find and make sense of in the foundational texts.

It is also the case that a good deal of the material that defines existentialism was written at a time when the term "man" or "mankind" was used as a metonym for all of humanity. Looking at these sources now demonstrates just how this practice both prioritised men in the overall picture of the world and also effaced the feminine by relegating women to a subaltern position. In light of this, there are a significant number of quotations in the book that reflect this dated language. Where one sees the word "man" deployed in this decidedly dated and unhelpful fashion, it is actually a useful prompt to consider the way in which language and our use of it shapes the world.

What use is this book?

This is a book about the business world ... but shouldn't be seen as a business book. It considers the living of our lives in the workplace and, in so doing, offers some critique of where we find ourselves in terms of that environment at this time. In that sense, the book offers both my analysis of where we presently find ourselves in relation to corporate life – but, at the same time, offers a suggested way of looking at that context.

To offer one example of how this might work in practice, in our weekly conversation that took place on 25 March 2025, my friend and colleague John Higgins and I ended up discussing an interview John had done around the topic of the "tempered radical" (Meyerson & Scully, 1995). Typically, we began our exploration of the topic on this occasion with a focus on organisational life – and how people might aspire to fulfil this abstracted role in the workplace. However, we later began to inquire into how a person existentially experiences the balance that lies at the heart of tempered radicalism, namely how can one be extremely and openly supportive of the place in which one finds oneself working while at the same time desperately wanting to change it for the better, as you perceive it.

To summarise, then, this work is not presented as a prescription but is instead a personal description of how I – and others with whom I have spoken – experience our existing when we are immersed in our working lives. Business books tend to offer a cut-and-dried solution to whatever issue they are looking to tackle, an approach to the world – and particularly the realm of business – that my friend Steve Hearsum challenges as being the pursuit of the illusion of a "silver bullet" that offers a quick fix (Hearsum, 2024). So, alongside the analysis, this book depicts a way of looking at and thinking about the world, which does not define what a person should do but instead offers insight into how a human agent might reflect differently on their experience and potentially discover for themselves new ways of existing in the world … particularly the world of work.

Hence, Chapter 7 supports an existential way of philosophising by reflecting back on the specific themes covered in each of the preceding chapters and suggesting one possible way in which a person could engage critically with their world of work – whether as an employee or as a manager/leader in that setting – and potentially identify for themselves another way of being in that realm.

Above all else, I hope that you enjoy reading this book and that in some way it inspires you. As ever with my writing, I do not see the publication of a volume as a full stop; instead I view it very much as the potential start of a conversation, where various voices can come together to talk about their experiences and their thinking, as part of an ongoing effort to understand the world better – and to work towards a better world.

Bibliography

Hearsum, S. (2024). *No Silver Bullet: Bursting the Bubble of the Organisational Quick Fix*. Brighton: Funky Otter Press.

Meyerson, D. E., & Scully, M. A. (1995, September–October). Tempered Radicalism and the Politics of Ambivalence and Change. *Organization Science, 6*(5), 585–600.

1 Thinking about being

The experience of schooling

The one thing I felt that school sought to teach me – from the first day at primary through to that final Friday in secondary school, which saw me desperately chasing around the corridors to find my form teacher so he could sign the chit that released me – was that I was stupid.

I raced out of those gates at the age of 16 with three O Levels to my name. I had managed a B grade in English. This did not feel to be a surprise. After all, in the second year there – what would now be called Year 8 – the pupils were arranged into a league table at the end of term for each subject studied. This reflected classroom achievement, marks from homework, and any test scores in that academic year. And I came first (as if learning was some sort of race), although – when announcing this fact to the whole class – my English teacher, Mr Taylor, could not help but openly express his surprise that I had somehow achieved this position.

I got a C in History – and, to my delight, had achieved the same grade in Physics. I was a poor student who struggled to see the value of formal education at that time and who found study difficult, particularly revision. I had entered the examination hall for that Physics paper pretty certain I was about to waste three valuable hours of my time. On that occasion, the limited number of topics to which I had paid attention as I went through the pretence of going back over what the school insisted I had learned all turned up in the questions.

I recall producing one solution to a question that focused on Joules as measurements of energy. I have no recollection now as to what I was asked

DOI: 10.4324/9781003592624-1

and what equation I had to use. But, in that moment, sitting in serried ranks in a grandiose high-ceilinged hall, it all fell into place. What I do remember from then, even now, is that I carefully showed working out, of course, and thereby generated the answer of 42.

As I left the exam when it was finished, I collared Marco, a smart kid from my class, and quizzed him as to the answer he had produced for this question. When he said that it was 42, I recall excitedly saying, 'Yes, that's what I got!' Because it was a subject that I had never excelled in, I was particularly pleased with this result when it finally came through, even though another paper on this topic with different questions covering different elements of the syllabus would not have seen me achieve a pass grade.

A week or so after the results had been released, I bumped into Mr Beddoes, my Physics teacher, in the school playground. Bristling with something akin to pride, I greeted him effusively. He smirked back at me and said, 'Cole! You got a C grade!' There was a momentary pause and I waited in silence for what I assumed would be the praise that would follow. Instead, he simply said, 'How on Earth did you manage that?' Feeling utterly deflated, I recall simply shrugging, turning on my heel, and walking away.

As for the other O levels for which I was entered, they came back as either F grades – a Fail – or even more impressively as a U grade, which meant Unclassified. Such a mark doubtless indicated that I had barely put pen to paper during the examination. One such subject was Russian, a class into which I had been placed despite declaring that I wanted to learn German. It was never explained why I had been bounced into this select group of not more than eight of us, although it was widely joked that we had been compelled to do this to keep the Russian teacher in a job. I cannot imagine for a moment that MI6 had targeted me as a potential recruit who would need an acquaintance with the language of our Cold War communist enemy. Moreover, the belief clearly held by my parents that I was never going to be any sort of success at school meant that they did not feel the need to intervene on my behalf and advocate for me to be able to study German, as I had requested.

I certainly have no memory whatsoever of sitting that Russian exam. Occasionally, I will count aloud from one to three in the language – or say 'Hello. It is a lamp.' I can still just about recognise the Cyrillic alphabet, so will say Russian words that happen to appear on TV. Did I produce an examination script of some form, full of badly written Russian characters? Was there an oral test? I simply don't recall.

Part of the problem was that I was distracted from schoolwork by the fact that I was being relentlessly bullied. This experience led me to truant extensively, particularly during my entire Fifth Year (or Year 11). I would turn up for morning and afternoon registration and then simply leave the school campus, which had a number of means of escape, none of which were gated, let alone locked.

On one occasion in the Fifth Year, I bumped into Mr Jones, the Russian teacher, outside the staff room as I was rushing to make my escape for the afternoon. 'Cole, I haven't seen you for ages. Are you better?' he asked, assuming that my absence from his tiny class of Russian students was due to ill health. 'Yes, sir,' I quickly responded, 'I'm better now.' And off he bumbled to his next class and off I went into Bromley town centre to hide out in the shops and eventually take an extraordinarily circuitous route home, which meant I could avoid those who meant to make my life a misery for their entertainment and those who – in some more psychopathic instances – actually intended to do me harm.

Alongside the belittlement of me by Messrs Taylor and Beddoes, I also suffered Mr Isaacs, a maths teacher whose hair was the colour of chalk dust and whose lessons consistently remained a mystery to me, no matter how hard I tried to focus and follow what it was he was saying. I would gloomily sit at the dining table in the evening, struggling to engage with the homework that he had set. At some point on each occasion, I would allow myself to recognise that – regardless of how long I sat and stared at the questions in the textbook – they were not going to make sense and I was going to struggle to put anything down, let alone the right answer.

The following day, I would dutifully hand in whatever it was I had been able to generate. Then came the ritual humiliation of Mr Isaacs descending from the dais on which his huge desk stood at the head of the class and prowling down the classroom with my homework held at arm's length and disdainfully dangling from his thumb and forefinger. When he reached my little desk, he would release his grip and the paper would flutter awkwardly down, as he pronounced for all to hear, 'Cole. Nought. Again!'

What I learned from school

Amidst the rows of shabby desks and uncomfortable chairs and the cavernous space of the assembly or sports hall, there exists a pervasive notion of what a good pupil looks like. This exemplary figure is shaped by two factors: their institutional behaviour and academic achievement. In respect to the former and at the most basic level, the ideal student is one who turns up on time and appears at school regularly. They are expected to behave in a way that means that they comply with all aspects of the disciplinary regime of the institution in which they find themselves.

This commitment shapes their behaviour so that they do not come to the attention of the teachers for any negative reason. In existentialist terms, this is the essential image of the acceptable individual, the individual as socially moulded being, created against a template of the perfect self. But existentialism takes issue with the view that there is some agreed model for being a human to which we should aspire or be defined by. Instead, the philosophy focuses on what it means to live one's life in a way that rejects this socially determined identity and recognises the freedom that exists outside of the clutches of the approved of norm.

In this form of freedom, our being is more than the sum of the choices we make in the midst of the hurly-burly of life, and is better understood as how we are in the world, as part of a wider engagement with what it means to be human in the world. We step out of the sometimes comforting restrictions that limit our identity to a social label and a hotchpotch of accidental or deliberate choices, and into a sense of unframed being as the ground on which we stand.

This is what is meant when people like Sartre declare that 'existence precedes essence', being before framing, which is a position strongly connected to atheistic existentialism and is usefully articulated by the assertion that 'Man is nothing else but that which he makes of himself' (Sartre, 1948/1973, p. 28). The self-making is part of the universal human experience. In the absence of God intervening to do the self-making on mankind's behalf, it is suggested that there cannot truly be any meaningful idea of something that might be called 'human nature', there is no divine or ideal template, no model pupil for us to aspire to or for authorities to impose on us.

It becomes not about the choices that some given sense of self exercises, instead it is about how a sense of self is chosen in the first place. Self-choosing comes before making choices, For Sartre every single one of us is separately involved in work where we 'choose ourselves', which in turn means that, through our own personal choosing, we are also in effect choosing for all humankind (Sartre, 1948/1973, p. 29). We are a collective of self-choosing beings.

This contests at least one notion of freedom, which sees it as the right to act in an unbridled fashion – and solely as an individual, apart from others without any common or shared task. This is the freedom promoted by libertarians, of course, but which can also be awkwardly discerned in some of the political positions that exist within contemporary Leftism. But, as we have seen, while Sartrean existentialism reminds us that choice resides with us individually – he also foregrounds how this individual choice cannot be considered solely from our individual perspective.

Returning to a consideration of the social habits that undermine this, let's go back to the classroom and how these forces inveigle their way into what we can find ourselves believing about our identity. Alongside the image of the ideal school student, shaped by compliance with demands arising from authority, there is a complimentary perspective in respect to academic achievement. When I came first in the class in English back in 1972, I sat on top of a pile of what might helpfully be called achievers: we did what was expected of us by the teachers in terms of handing in work, revising, and sitting exams. Looking back on that now, I realise how well it demonstrates Michel Foucault's argument that a move from *sovereign* to *disciplinary power* is shaped in particular by the power/knowledge nexus of which he speaks so lucidly (Foucault, 1991), where what counts as knowledge is wrapped up with regimes of authority which authorises and normalises certain ways and forms of knowing.

By way of a more practical explanation of this, when I did my teacher training in the late 1980s, we were advised that the classrooms in which we worked could be said to be segmented thus: there would be five students who stood out as stars, who we would end up actively seeking to encourage; there would be five who were disinterested in what school had to offer and who we would need to closely supervise in order to manage their potential disruptiveness; and a mass of 20 others, who would end up being largely invisible.

The data that defines these three groups – drawn from things like school registers and various grades – has an important philosophical effect: it categorises the central 20 as 'normal' – and, in so doing, thereby inadvertently creates a category of the Other. Power arises in light of how we then think of normalcy and the outliers. This is especially pronounced when one looks at the statistical model of a bell curve: normalcy is defined at the heart of such a diagram, while the tails on either side of the graph are where people are Othered.

How come I am writing about this in the present tense when it is nigh on 50 years since I escaped school? Simply, talking to my young son about his day-to-day experience of primary school – in particular, Key Stage 2 – suggests that little, if anything, has changed. The focus is very heavily on the Standard Assessment Tests (SATs), which are a testing regime that is more accurately described as National Curriculum Assessment (Whetton, 2009), accompanied by normalised behavioural regimes in the classroom. This framework arose out of Thatcherism and enjoyed a continuity in terms of New Labour's adherence to the ideas of New Public Management, particularly in respect to introducing consumerist notions into public services (Gruening, 2001) and generating league tables of providers to support this, a practice that is contested by many in terms of what people are actually seeing in such data (Goldstein & Leckie, 2008).

Speaking in class remains unacceptable, other than when the teacher is choreographing the classroom and invites people to talk out loud – or, slightly more rarely, with one another. Where the idea of teams working together is fetishised in corporate settings (Cole, 2020, pp. 96–109), it looks to me as though schooling – with what appears to be an expectation that educational activities need to be undertaken in a state of isolation alongside a concentration on grades achieved by individual activity – is shaped by a managerialism where a person's individual performance is paramount, notwithstanding the social context in which they work.

This roughly speaking still fits within the overall view of what is called the *correspondence principle*, which persuasively argues from a Marxist perspective that school mirrors the experience of the world of work – and so is the main means through which we are inducted into the capitalist workplace and by which the outlook and practices therein are reproduced over time (Bowles & Gintis, 1976). Hence, while the workplace remains fixated on the idea of people working in 'teams', a cursory glance at most performance appraisal systems sees a strong focus on what the individual does and how they do it.

How is this 'correspondent' schooling regime achieved? Bowles and Gintis suggest several ways. School is written through with power and is structured as a hierarchy, just as we might see in a traditional corporate setting. Schoolwork is undertaken in order to attain a reward – one submits an essay or an examination script so that a teacher evaluates and offers you a mark – which is akin to the exchange that occurs at work in respect to being paid a wage. And there is a *hidden curriculum*, which subtly encourages us to embrace docility: we become uniform, often through the wearing of a uniform; subjects we study are segmented; and we learn about timekeeping, attendance, taking our turns, queueing, and accepting our position amidst a mass of others.

The structure of formal education – and the workplace, into which school seeks to ensure that we are equipped to graduate – limits our human spirit, in particular our unique capacity as human beings to engage with the world, experience a time-limited freedom therein, and make myriad choices on a moment-by-moment basis throughout the duration of our lives.

The world of work

No sooner had I sprinted free from the clutches of school that Friday lunchtime, than I found myself being driven in dad's car to the Job Centre in

Bromley. He and I perused the cards attached to various boards until Dad lifted one off and passed it to me, with the observation, 'Here you are, that'll do'. A jewellery store in Woolwich wanted a shop assistant. I had no sense what this would entail but felt sure it would be better than school, so I took the card to the desk, where the person phoned the shop and I was told they would interview me right now if I could get there. Dad indicated that would be fine, so we were soon on our way.

The interview – such as it was – took place at the counter in the shop. I don't recall what I was asked, but I clearly gave a good account of myself as I was told I could start on Monday. Dad then drove us back to Bromley, where he lent me some money to buy a polyester blue pinstripe three-piece suit and a fat tie with peacocks on it.

The commute was something of a challenge, especially in the winter: there were two possible routes, both of which involved catching two buses. The one I preferred was to catch the 94 from Bromley Common to Petts Wood and then race across the railway bridge to what was called Station Square, where occasional 161s from Woolwich would end their journey and turn around.

One frosty morning, I stood looking down the long, straight, and busy road, waiting for the red smudge of a London bus to appear in the misty distance. I was standing right by the bus stop, which had a litter bin attached to it. My eyes were drawn to its very full contents. Near the top, it was possible to discern a paperback book that someone had thrown away. I peered in to see what it was – and saw the author's name, Jean-Paul Sartre.

Despite my apparently dismal school career, I knew enough to recognise it – and to realise that he was a highly respected French writer. I was also taken by the fact that the book looked to be a collection of short stories, under the title *Intimacy*, also the name of the first story in the collection (Sartre, 1916). Overcoming years of parental voices telling me to 'Get out of the dirt', I dipped my hand into the bin and plucked out the book. I tried to do it surreptitiously as I was aware that others were around me, all of us waiting for the bus – but this act on my part signalled the start of an altogether different journey to the one I was about to take on the Number 94.

I read that book cover to cover in a couple of days. I remember thinking that – regardless of what school had taught me about myself – I couldn't be as stupid as they had made out if I was able to read something like this. I threw myself into reading his other works, including *The Roads to Freedom* trilogy – and crucially the novel *Nausea*, a superb fictional exploration of the issues that arose out of Sartre's particular take on existentialist philosophy (Sartre, 2020).

At some level, the experiences of the protagonist in *Nausea* – a character called Roquentin – resonated deeply with me. I quickly absorbed the thinking that undergirded the story and felt that it made sense through my life thus far and to my life right now. This, then, is the point where I became fascinated by what is talked about as not so much a philosophy as a style of philosophising (Macquarrie, 1973, p. 14).

Living through a crisis

At some point early in March 2020, I found myself in Sainsbury's, doing the family weekly shop. I can quite easily call to mind an eidetic memory of things that I experienced in that moment. Specifically, I peered down one aisle and realised that there was not a single packet of pasta left in the store; similarly, elsewhere in the shop, I saw that there was literally nothing on the shelves where the toilet paper should have been. The frightening illness about which the world was constantly speaking at that time was one thing to worry about, but there was a separate concern in terms of whether the arrival of this sinister coronavirus was about to turn the world on its head and destroy all the things that I took for granted in terms of living in a society like the UK.

At the end of that month, it was my 60th birthday. We had planned a party, which had to be abandoned because we could not see how it was going to be sensible to bring a large group of people together when a horrible disease was rife – and then because the first lockdown began on 23 March. The appearance of a pandemic ahead of that milestone birthday, alongside a wider sense for me that things could very quickly fall apart under the pressure of Covid-19, left me feeling deeply shaken. In fact, I felt unwell, unable to function.

I had a remote consultation with my GP, where they diagnosed that I was suffering from anxiety. So profound was the impact of this condition on me that the doctor signed me off work for an initial fortnight – and then for a further two weeks. In this instance, I was experiencing anxiety through its signs and symptoms: I felt constantly tense and on edge, with myriad physical manifestations arising in me repeatedly. I was haunted by thoughts of catastrophe, which left me both panicked and irritated. I could not focus on anything; I felt lost in my own thoughts, most of which were intensely gloomy. The dark and silence of bedtime would often trigger a deep sense of terror in me, which made sleeping increasingly difficult.

This, of course, is a clinical description of how I experienced anxiety at that time – and, to a lesser extent, how it affects me still today. It pivots around the two fears outlined above: firstly, there felt to be the possibility of life cut short by an illness that was not (and is still not) fully understood.

Alongside this, there was our participation in the largest clinical trial known in history, where speedily developed vaccines that responded to the global crisis were administered without the luxury of a decent time span to explore all of their efficacies and possible problems.

This is not to subscribe to a conspiracy theory; instead, it is merely to recognise that the circumstances appeared at that time to demand a quick reaction, so quick, in fact, that it was not going to be possible to cross all of the 'T's and dot all of the 'I's. There is much to learn from our experience of this major upheaval – and there is one facet of contemporary thinking that really needs to be challenged by the reflections and inquiry into what happened: we need – once and for all – to abandon the quaint notion that the world is comprehensively knowable and predictably certain.

Here is our opportunity to critically engage with some of the myths that inhibit our thinking and create false certainties for humankind. This means finally accepting that the idea that 'all is fixable' is an absurd position to hold. Linked to this, we need to abandon the notion that perfection is the state that we should constantly pursue. Lastly, we must set aside the conceit that there is just one right way of doing things (Cole & Higgins, 2022). In practice, as people sought to navigate the complexity of the pandemic, they were required to think and behave very differently. The phrase 'Building the plane while flying it' has been used to describe this experience and one piece of research that focused on healthcare leaders in Australia makes the following observations:

> The COVID-19 pandemic created unique situations that many healthcare leaders had not previously encountered. The broad nature of the pandemic response not only required leadership of an operational health service, but it also required leadership during a crisis with no clear end, and in roles that were newly defined to many. Leadership roles during a prolonged crisis are expected to be the commander and decision makers at the same time as being participative leaders that listen and build relationships between different groups to work collaboratively to solve the crisis.
>
> (McKenna, et al., 2023, p. 23)

From an existentialist perspective, this demonstrates that a reliance on something seen to be an essential nature runs into difficulty when confronted by the infinite contingency of human existence. It is possible to suggest that, prior to the arrival of the coronavirus, people were transfixed by the idea of how best to achieve the textbook definition of the 'leader'. With the arrival of Covid-19, however, we see people forced to engage moment by moment in the actuality of 'leadership' as practice rather than a formalised notion of being a leader. They faced unknown and uncertain circumstances, were compelled to make sense of the situation faced in that moment, and thence engaged in multiple choices – some big, some small – that defined both them and humankind more generally. This is a prime example of existence preceding essence, leading before leadership.

The second fear was that the veneer of civilisation was about to disappear under the multiple pressures that the presence of the virus around the globe was creating. In the earliest stages, it looked as though Covid had the potential to disrupt society in the sorts of way we have become accustomed to seeing in films like *28 Days Later* (2002). It's not that its victims would become zombies – but rather that our collective life itself would become zombified, given the impact that this disease was set to have on all of the things we rely on, such as food supplies, healthcare, and public safety.

Existentialism and anxiety

It is suggested that 'In existentialism, anxiety and concepts such as anguish, fear, and dread point to a human condition stemming from freedom' (Mui, 2013, p. 10). We suddenly find ourselves in the world and are faced with a freedom that requires us to make choices, in a place where there is no meaning other than that which we create for ourselves. Small wonder, then, that anxiety is seen to be an intrinsic and inescapable part of the human condition.

Kierkegaard – in terms of his philosophical investigations of the tensile relationship between human agency and adherence to religious faith, which can be seen as his attempt to 'awaken readers to the urgency of their lives – ultimately, to their awareness of sin and desire for redemption' (Michelman, 2010, p. 201) – offers the following insight into how central anxiety is to the very act of being a human:

> Anxiety may be compared with dizziness. He whose eye happens to look down into the yawning abyss becomes dizzy. But what is the reason for this? It is just as much in his own eye as in the abyss, for suppose he had not looked down. Hence anxiety is the dizziness of freedom, which emerges when the spirit wants to posit the synthesis and freedom looks down into its own possibility, laying hold of finiteness to support itself. Freedom succumbs in this dizziness. Further than this, psychology cannot and will not go. In that very moment everything is changed, and freedom, when it again rises, sees that it is guilty.
>
> (Kierkegaard, 1844/1980, p. 61)

This freedom that is intrinsic to our very existence and is ever-present, despite what we see as the constraints that hinder us from making the choices we might actually want to make, is unsurprisingly dizzying when we confront it. In existentialism, it is suggested that we spend a lot of time distracting ourselves from the myriad choices that we have within our grasp moment by moment across our lives. Within this body of thought, to recognise and engage with that freedom is to live authentically; to turn away from that freedom and pretend it is not there is to be in bad faith, as Sartre describes it.

What does Sartre mean by living in bad faith? He offers an example of a woman who agrees to go out on a date. She has an awareness of the intentions and expectations of the person with whom she is going to spend time over dinner. That cognisance means that she has already accepted that at some point she will have to decide how she feels about this arrangement, but she puts off that choice as it seems too difficult in this moment.

The woman hears what her date is saying but opts to ignore the clear subtexts in much of their conversation, taking things totally at face value. And should her date reach across the restaurant table and place their hand on hers, she is immediately confronted with a binary decision: leave her hand there to preserve the moment or withdraw it, which would shatter the apparent harmony of the situation. If she refuses actively to make a decision either way, she has still decided, as her hand remains in that of the date – and seems to suggest she has responded positively to this advance. But her decision has taken place in bad faith (Sartre, 1965/1993, pp. 160–162).

In existentialism, anxiety is not merely a reaction to the world and its circumstances, as I experienced in 2020. Instead, drawing on the work of Heidegger, one commentator notes that 'You are … alienated from the world, not because you do not know what surrounds you, but rather because the world offers you nothing in terms of which to make sense of your own life' (Blattner, 2024, p. 125). The triumvirate of existentialist writers who focus on anxiety as a key notion in the philosophy are Kierkegaard, Heidegger, and Sartre – and, notwithstanding the fact that Kierkegaard proceeds from a foundation of Christian faith, both the others acknowledge their debt to the Dane. But the three are linked by the fact that they all see anxiety to be 'revelatory of the human condition' (Macquarrie, 1973, p. 165).

When I found the courage to consider my experience of anxiety and what looked to have triggered it, a large part of it derived from the fact that the peaceful and reassuring post-war period had been suddenly and profoundly disrupted by a deadly virus. As noted earlier, John Higgins and I had interrogated some of the key notions that undergirded that extended period of stability, chief of which was that everything was thought to be fixable. It has been interesting to me to contrast my intellectual engagement in denying and disrupting this ideological conceit – and the simple fact that, on careful reflection, I can now see how powerfully reassuring that perspective was to me at a deeply personal and existential level. I am compelled in light of this to recognise the bad faith in which I was living in that regard.

As the supposed fixability of the world frayed and fell away in response to a tiny virus whizzing around the globe, I was confronted by the simple fact that the world is, in fact, uncertain and unknowable, something that I struggled to accept. Yet this was something I shared with people with whom I worked across health care in London as I spoke with them regarding the virtues of systemic thinking and working. It brought home to me how deeply woven into our being are these takes on the world – and they operate there at a profoundly emotional level, even as we publicly denounce them at an intellectual one. To think of both our personal and work lives as certain, knowable, and always fixable is deeply reassuring but wholly lacking in substance, if we take the time to reflect on instances in life like the arrival of Covid-19.

I was also aware that the pandemic had triggered something that was already nascent inside me, namely a profound sense of temporality. This existential term is an active acknowledgment of the fact that, from the moment we are born, we are faced with the knowledge of our own finitude. For most of my life, I have worked extraordinarily hard not to face this simple fact, despite having fished that Sartre book out of the bin and then going on to engage with the ideas of existentialism as they appeared in the works of a wide range of writers. My own bad faith led me to delude myself by always carrying in my mind's eye a vision of myself when I was 17 years old.

Approaching my 60th birthday, that mental image began to break up like the picture on an old-fashioned TV with its signal disrupted. I was compelled to consider my finitude – and this at a time when something arrived in the world that was minute and murderous. I recall a conversation at some point in 2022, where a very supportive mental health nurse at my GP surgery listened intently to me as I described my gloomy focus on the dark side of the pandemic and wondered aloud why I had become so preoccupied by this. 'It's no surprise, really,' she calmly intoned. 'Over the past couple of years, we have been confronted with death daily through the media. And we have been constantly told that we risk being killed by others – and that, at the same time, we are likely to kill them.'

Seeking help

While the GP had – with some reluctance – signed me off from work at the very start of the crisis and my poor reaction to it, there was little chance of accessing the mental health support I so desperately needed. He said he wouldn't be able to make a referral to my local NHS mental health trust but that I would be able to self-refer. I was in no fit state to challenge this absurdity at the time – but now struggle to understand the clinical logic underpinning this, if indeed there was such a rationale.

Feeling desperate, I completed the form on the Trust's website. Shortly afterwards, I was contacted and an online assessment session was scheduled. A very considerate and efficient health-care worker talked me through a set of structured questions, which included one that asked whether I was considering suicide. I remember saying that it was fear of death that had left me feeling mentally unwell, so there was no way I would give this a passing thought. But this, of course, is an algorithmic question that sees you move up the waiting list if you respond to it in a positive (suicidal) fashion.

My assessor reassured me at the end of the session that she was pretty certain that the Trust would be able to offer some assistance. A week or so later, following a conversation with a supervisor, she contacted me again to say that, whilst I was unwell, it was not severe enough to give me access to treatment. Instead, I was sent away with a list of charitable providers, who provided talking therapies at prices below market rate. I remember thinking at that point that the NHS as a model of socialised medicine, free at the point of need, had disappeared, in light of its signal failure to offer me the support that for the first time in my entire life I was reaching out to receive.

I arranged further assessments with two of the providers on the list. At one, a local branch of a very large mental health charity, the person assessing me ran through the positive array of services they offered, including group walks in the country, workshops, and financial guidance. Eventually, she said that they offered counselling and I promptly said that this was exactly what I was eager to access. There came a pause. 'Ah. OK', she said hesitantly. 'Unfortunately, there is a 10–12 month waiting list.'

The sole advantage of this failure to offer any kind of meaningful support through the NHS, let alone treatment, at a time when my mental health was in shreds, was that it allowed me to reflect on what sort of assistance I would most value in terms of where I found myself and how I felt. Suddenly, a thread emerged in the rich fabric of time between that copy of *Intimacy* in the litter bin and my deep discomfiture in face of advancing years and the continued presence of a deadly disease. I did not just need a psychotherapist, I needed one who approached their work from an existential position. And I was lucky enough to find a brilliant practitioner called Malcolm to whom I turned privately for the support that I so desperately needed.

Conveyor belt therapy

I also recognised that I needed support that flowed from being in human-to-human contact, as opposed to immersion in a structured framework of activity, such as Cognitive Behavioural Therapy (CBT) which is the default option in the vast majority of instances where people present with depression or anxiety. I am, of course, aware that this style of intervention is extremely effective for a good many people, an effect borne out in research on the method's efficacy (Butler et al., 2006), although the meta-analytic methodology used to generate these positive assessments has its limitations (Wampold, et al., 2017). However, that does not mean that it is acceptable and applicable in every instance – and it does not recognise a theoretical contestation of the approach that exists.

For example, there is an issue as to the range of practices that can reasonably fall under the broad CBT umbrella. However, a useful starting point is that 'Cognitive behavioural therapy … focuses on the way people *think and act* in order to help them overcome their emotional and behavioural problems' (Willson & Branch, 2006, p. 9) [Emphasis added]. This definition offers insight into its critique, highlighting the way in which such practices reduce mental distress to something that can simply be reframed and casually set aside.

CBT is not interested in why the client is depressed or anxious, two states that can very easily flow simply from the peaks and troughs of the human condition; it is driven by the medical model in mental health, so these two states are taken to be illnesses that need to be cured. Hence, one critic of the approach observes that:

> If you feel depressed say, then it is because you have not yet understood how to take control of your inner life. This is where CBT will come to the rescue: it will explain to you how your inner life works; it will then train you in techniques to control its workings. If, after all this, you still cannot control your inner life despite having understood the mechanism, then either this is of your choosing, or it is because you are still in the grip of your mental illness.
>
> (Dalal, 2018, p. 6)

This underscores the fact that CBT is seen to be something that concerns itself exclusively with the individual and their positivity, while completely neglecting the social. It is founded on an essentialist image of the 'well' person. Linked to this is the fact that these interventions can be seen to be medicalising the human condition, which is why CBT needs to be viewed alongside an existentialist view of the world. The contrast could not be sharper: CBT is seeking to fix people because it assumes that something has become diseased or broken. Existentialism proceeds from the position that we arrive in life and need then to find our way through it, which requires us to recognise that life itself is something of a challenge – but one to which we can adapt.

As one practising existential therapist notes, 'Existential anxiety is interested in attempting to create meaning while living an uncertain life as a human, moving from birth to death through all of the cycles of human existence' (Cummings-Knight, 2024, p. 24). This stands in sharp contrast to notions of adjustments of individual behaviour. It denies the very idea that there is something rooted in us that needs to be actively tackled, focusing instead on our sense-making and wayfinding throughout our ontogeny, the entire course of the life of an organism from conception through to demise.

CBT also propagates the myth of controllability, not least because it is suggested that it is sustained by what is referred to as 'hyper-rationality', a foundation that is said to emerge out of psychology's dogged fixation on scientism (the fetishisation and ideologisation of the scientific method that leads to the assumption that it can be universally applied to all circumstances) and being seen to be a scientific discipline (Dalal, 2018, pp. 1–10). To that extent, it subscribes to the myth that 'all is fixable', a nonsensical position noted earlier in this chapter (Cole & Higgins, 2022). This is an attempt, then, to scientise the complexity of life – and goes on to suggest somewhat absurdly that this complexity is in some fashion manageable, simply by forcing ourselves to change our behaviours.

In light of this, an intersection is perceived between three contemporary disciplines and policies, all of which are undergirded by this notion of hyper-rationality, something seen to arise out of 'physics envy'. Unlike the philosophical notion of rationalism, which underpinned the Enlightenment, hyper-rationality has a tendency to elevate the scientism that is so central to it that fresh thinking and intellectual challenge are effectively closed down (Dalal, 2018, p. 3). These three are said to be the political approach known as neo-liberalism, its associated economic practice called New Public Management, and psychological science. They don't just interconnect, they actively reinforce one another (Dalal, 2018, p. 5)

It is suggested that Canada – specifically Ontario – offers a remarkable case study in this regard. In terms of a province-wide initiative to provide access to CBT back in 2020, it is argued that this initiative can be seen to be underwritten by neo-liberal ideology in terms of the way in which the intervention is grounded on contestable notions of individual responsibility, productivity, and recovery (Smith, 2022, p. 3).

To further reinforce the tension noted earlier, this analysis asserts that 'CBT programs place the burden of change on the individual, rather than the collective …, as though this strategy can undo trauma and systemic harm', which the author notes will encompass experiences of both abuse in all of its manifestations and oppression arising out of the socio-economic constructs of the society in which we live (Smith, 2022, p. 5). Had I opted for CBT to address my anxiety, the focus would have been on managing the symptoms rather than considering, as I currently do in my weekly 50-minute session with Malcolm, the origins of the language of anxiety, and seeing it as a normal feature of the human condition, from an existentialist perspective.

Meanwhile, it seems that our contemporary focus on health and well-being – something endlessly highlighted in corporate settings at this time – is not an altruistic response to anxiety, notwithstanding the motivations of those involved at the grassroots in delivering this area of work, but is closely linked to getting people back to work as soon as possible and ensuring that their productivity is maximised. This seems particularly apparent in a substantial review of the efficacy of a range of workplace-based interventions around mental well-being, which opens with the following statement:

> According to the most recently available Labour Force Survey for 2004–2005, 509,000 individuals in the UK believed they were suffering from stress, depression or anxiety and these conditions were caused or made worse by their current or past work. This resulted in an estimated 12.8 million working days lost with an average of 30.9 days off over a 12-month period. Those employed in the public sector had some of the highest rates of self-reported stress, anxiety and depression. In particular those with heavy workloads, tight deadlines, lack of support at work, in a threatening environment are recognised as being at an increased risk of stress, depression or anxiety. This review aims to determine which workplace interventions are effective and cost-effective in improving mental wellbeing.
>
> (Graveling et al., 2008, p. i)

A commitment to cost-effectiveness is explicit here, while the focus on getting people speedily back to work is apparent in the quantification of workdays lost, as opposed to the actual experiences of the people involved. Moreover, there is an internal logic to using something like CBT to address the conditions reported by the people mentioned here. But the explicit reference to a context of intense workplace pressure as a central causal factor reminds us that an existentialist approach to the issue will be more productive, in terms of inviting people to articulate the impact of workplace expectations on them – and how addressing the lived context would likely have a more immediate, long-lasting, and effective impact on well-being at work.

In the far too often inhumane world of Human Resources (HR), you can find this openly stated. For example, you do not need to look far to find HR people expressing concern about employees experiencing poor well-being in terms of its impact on their managers and organisational effectiveness, explicitly related to issues of individual performance and productivity – and how that might impact a company's competitive advantage (Kowalski & Loretto, 2017). The only interest here is ensuring people are 'fit to work' – and it should also remind us that 'Attempting to address poor wellbeing from within the institutional framework that has created it inevitably leads to seeing it as partly or wholly a problem of reduced productivity since this is workers' function' (Watson et al., 2023, p. 449). That is a vicious circle that urgently needs to be broken.

Choices along the way

The choice I made to dip my hand into that bin full of rubbish felt at the time – and for a long time afterwards – to be a minor decision on my part. Slowly, though, its ramifications became more apparent. I lifted the book from the bin and read it promptly; that experience and my reflections on it helped me adjust the view that I had of myself. It led me to read more – and more widely – than I thought it was possible for me to do. It gave me confidence to step into spaces which I had been taught to assume – at home and in school – were foreign to me; and it saw me make more choices which could not have opened up, had I not made that initial choice.

I concede that going back into full-time education was a choice – but choosing seemed to stop immediately thereafter, as I found myself on an escalator, being distracted by the motion as the stairway moved up from one course to another, until I momentarily stepped off when I completed my teacher training … only to rejoin it later.

That initial ride up from the ground floor saw me step off at the top into the world of work, where I assumed the silent and compliant role that my father had said was essential to success. I took on the role of a corporate drone for pretty much 25 years, doing as I was told and barely taking time to question anything that I was asked to do. Instead of engaging critically with where I had landed and what I did there, I simply slipped into the role of docile obedience.

I cannot now recall whether I articulated any concerns about what I was doing and how I was doing outside of work. That said, my dear friend Dave – who worked for many years behind the scenes in one of the high street's extremely well-known food stores – used to speak when we socialised about a mutual acquaintance with whom he worked who would describe his day-to-day corporate experience as 'Shadow boxing in the fog while someone throws shit at you from a helicopter'. So I feel certain that I did speak with people I knew about just how grim organisational life could be on occasions.

Prior to going back into education, I had been a Labour Party activist and a trade union steward. I reflect on that period a good deal, as it offered me the opportunity to actively and positively experience myself in the world – but equally it was a time when I thought very little and merely followed the crowd, in terms of both thought and action. I was tacitly complying with a range of what were seen as essential factors, a constellation of thoughts and practices that were deemed to define what it meant to be a left-wing activist. Choices were made for me by the circumstances in which I enthusiastically steeped myself. Paradoxically, I chose not to make choices.

My personal experience here finds a strong echo in Sartre's intellectual efforts to reconcile the existentialist perspective that he crafted – distinguished by its focus on individual freedom and choice – with the crude collectivism and determinism of Marxism (Sartre, 2008). Despite his efforts to craft a bridge, in particular through his publication *Search for a Method*, to connect his philosophical thought with his political activism, which included going onto the streets to peddle a Maoist rag, the two positions still stand at a notable distance from one another (Sartre, 1963).

This leads one commentator to declare that the philosopher cannot realistically be thought of as a Marxist, notwithstanding this supposed shift in perspective. Amidst many points of contention, the following offers just one indication as to how existentialism and Marxism stand firmly apart:

> For Sartre, the only way to fully live in freedom was for human beings with similar fundamental projects to band together. However, Sartre, the eternal realist, did not believe in any quick waning of the state and state power. This first political philosophy that Sartre ever developed was emphatically not a Marxist, but an anarchist one. Nothing proves

> this better than the fact that state power worried him more than its economic counterpart. The term 'existentialist Marxism' would definitely not have found favor with Sartre in the years before his death.
> (Betschart, 2019, p. 84)

For me, the two perspectives enjoy a symbiotic relationship. The collective is a social space that supports people to engage in dialogue and explore ideas. This is where a connected and panoramic intelligence can arise in response to our jointly faced problems, challenges, and ambitions. But the collective can only exist and truly function when a human agent makes that profound and active decision to join it. Thereafter, in an ideal circumstance, those two perspectives should interact in a reflexive and productive way, by which I mean:

1. The *individual* should not merely surrender themselves to the collective but must keep their connection with it under review. It is important not to be unthinkingly absorbed into any form of group, so involvement is something to which we ought to commit actively on a moment-by-moment basis as a check and balance on the group. This is where our existentialist freedom emerges perhaps most noticeably, as we opt to merge ourselves with others to gain the benefit of togetherness, meaning both collective intelligence and collective action … but, at the same time, maintain our critical capacities in order to choose to leave or challenge that collective, if we experience concerns about it.
2. The *collective* must offer space and time for people to come together in a way that is mindful not merely of the power that surrounds that group … but also the power inside the group that the dynamics of people coming together and engaging in conversation generates. It must recognise that human beings when coming together will often fractionate, allowing factions to arise. The collective in that sense is like a magnet, able to strongly attract and repulse at the same time.

Trading old traps for new ones

In July 2023, I stepped free of salaried work, somewhere I had spent just over 40 years of my life. This was not an easy decision: I liked and deeply respected the people with whom I worked most closely and at that time – for the first time in my career – had found work that truly engaged me, gave me great pleasure to do, and at which I seemed to be quite good.

But I was far from content with where I found myself doing that work – and increasingly found it difficult not to express my opinion in that regard. And, as most people in corporate life are aware, the public invitation to speak up that comes from the upper echelons of our organisations is too often darkly balanced by a profound intolerance of what people might then end up saying.

On the first working day after I had left, I was genuinely elated by an intense feeling of liberty. In all my years at work, I had signally failed to properly acknowledge how constraining corporate life had been. But every bright light can cast particularly dark shadows. And, for me, that freedom was a powerfully positive sensation but, at the same time, I was also suddenly confronted by the fact that this now meant that it was exclusively down to me rather than my paid employment to create meaning and structure in my life. This responsibility had always been there, of course, although it is far more easily avoided when we allow the structures of paid work to frame our lives.

Suddenly, I could sense an arc that ran from Sartre in the bin and my subsequent immersion in existentialist thought, through my ongoing attempts to 'loosen the grip' of my anxiety (to apply the helpful phrase that is used in my therapy) to being confronted with my freedom as I stepped away from salaried employment into a freelance role. I had presumed for 40 years that I was at liberty to do as I chose – but the following exposition offers insight into its illusory nature:

> Sartre has likewise written about the waiter who is not free. The waiter … is not in a prison – at least, not in a visible one. But secretly, invisibly, in his inner being, the waiter has never been free. He has long since surrendered his freedom, his personal integrity, to the image of being a waiter. He enters the room a little too much like a waiter. He carries his tray with an expertness that betrays the fact that he is a waiter, that more than anything else in the world he is a waiter. He is a waiter before he is a man. His individualism has been lost to the profession of catering. He has conformed to the image of what other people conceive of a waiter as being.
>
> (Killinger, 1961, p. 304)

In this reflective chapter, a range of concepts crucial to existentialism have been highlighted, including temporality, freedom and choice, anxiety, and meaning making. I will now explore being at work – by which I mean spending time in that context and existing as a person – through those notions derived from existentialist thought. This opening chapter is a personal exploration of my life in terms of thought and experience; I deliberately chose to approach it in this fashion in order to own the topic, rather than distance myself from it in terms of abstract theorising. Like Sartre's waiter, I have lived under the illusion of liberty.

But now I want to acknowledge my circumstances – and potentially those of many others – and consider how existentialism might serve to humanise the workplace, which is the place where a good many of us spend a significant amount of our time. Beyond that humanising ambition, I want to offer people a means by which they might access the confidence needed to acknowledge and embrace their existence – and thereby, like Sartre's waiter, move to take ownership of their personhood.

Bibliography

Betschart, A. (2019). Sartre was not a Marxist. *Sartre Studies International, 25*(2), 77–91.

Blattner, W. (2024). *Heidegger's Being and Time* (2nd ed.). London: Bloomsbury Academic.

Bowles, S., & Gintis, H. (1976). *Schooling in Capitalist America: Educational Reform and the Contradictions of Economic Life.* New York: Haymarket Books.

Butler et al. (2006). The empirical status of cognitive-behavioral therapy: A review of meta-analyses. *Clinical Psychology Review, 26*(1), 17–31.

Cole, M. (2020). *Radical Organisation Development.* Abingdon: Routledge.

Cole, M., & Higgins, J. (2022). *Leadership Unravelled: The Faulty Thinking behind Modern Management.* Abingdon: Routledge.

Cummings-Knight, J. (2024). The Anxious Generation. *Hermaneutic Circular* (October), 24–25.

Dalal, F. (2018). *CBT: The Cognitive Behavioural Tsunami – Managerialism, Politics and the Corruptions of Science.* Abingdon: Routledge.

Foucault, M. (1991). *Discipline and Punish: The Birth of the Prison.* London: Penguin.

Goldstein, H., & Leckie, G. (2008). School league tables: What can they really tell us? *Significance* (June), 67–69.

Graveling, R. A., Crawford, J. O., Cowie, H., Amati, C., & Vohra, S. (2008). *A Review of Workplace Interventions that Promote Mental Wellbeing in the Workplace.* Edinburgh: Institute of Occupational Medicine (IOM).

Gruening, G. (2001). Origin and theoretical basis of New Public Management. *International Public Management Journal, 4*, 1–25.

Kierkegaard, S. (1844/1980). *The Concept of Anxiety: A Simple Psychologically Orienting Deliberation on the Dogmatic Issue of Hereditary Sin.* Princeton, NJ: Princeton University Press.

Killinger, J. (1961). Existentialism and Human Freedom. *The English Journal, 50*(5), 303–313.

Kowalski, T. H., & Loretto, W. (2017). Well-being and HRM in the changing workplace. *The International Journal of Human Resource Management, 28*(16), 2229–2255.

Macquarrie, J. (1973). *Existentialism.* Harmondsworth: Penguin.

McKenna, K., Bouchoucha, S., Redley, B., & Hutchinson, A. (2023). "Building the plane while flying it": Reflections on pandemic preparedness and response; an organisational case study. *BMC Health Services Research, 23*(940), 1–25. doi:https://doi.org/10.1186/s12913-023-09874-x

Michelman, S. (2010). *The A to Z of Existentialism.* Lanham, MD: The Scarecrow Press.

Mui, C. L. (2013). Anxiety. In H. Gordon (Ed.), *Dictionary of Existentialism* (pp. 10–12). Abingdon: Routledge.

Sartre, J.-P. (1916). *Intimacy and Other Stories.* London: Neville Spearman Ltd. Retrieved 1 October 2024, from https://archive.org/details/in.ernet.dli.2015.147679

Sartre, J.-P. (1948/1973). *Existentialism & Humanism.* London: Eyre Methuen.

Sartre, J.-P. (1963). *Search for a Method.* New York: Alfred A Knopf.

Sartre, J.-P. (1965/1993). *Essays in Existentialism.* (W. Baskin, Ed.) New York: Citadel Press, Kensington Publishing Corp.

Sartre, J.-P. (2008). The itinerary of a thought. In *Between Existentialism and Marxism* (pp. 33–63). London: Verso.

Sartre, J.-P. (2020). *Nausea.* London: Penguin Classics.

Smith, S. (2022). Neoliberalism and mental health care in Ontario: A critique of internet-based cognitive behavioural therapy. *Canadian Journal of Disability Studies, 11*(1), 1–25. Retrieved 10 October 2024, from https://cjds.uwaterloo.ca/index.php/cjds/article/view/849

Wampold, B. E., Flückiger, C., Del Re, A. C., Yulish, N. E., Frost, N. D., Pace, B. T.,... Hilsenroth, M. J. (2017). In pursuit of truth: A critical examination of meta-analyses of cognitive behavior therapy. *Psychotherapy Research, 27*(1), 14–32.

Watson, D., Wallace, J., Land, C., & Patey, J. (2023). Re-organising wellbeing: Contexts, critiques and contestations of dominant wellbeing narratives. *Organization, 30*(3), 441–452.

Whetton, C. (2009). EDITORIAL: National curriculum assessment in England: How well has it worked? Perspectives from the UK, Europe and beyond. *Educational Research, 51*(2), 131–135.

Willson, R., & Branch, R. (2006). *Cognitive Behavioural Therapy for Dummies.* Chichester: John Wiley & Sons.

Being free in the firm 2

Good evening, I'll be your waiter tonight

In company meetings, we are very often called upon to introduce ourselves. In most cases, we start with our name, the thing that tethers us to the reality that surrounds us. But very quickly thereafter, we share a job title, either by saying it aloud to those physically around us or by typing it into the chatbox of a virtual meeting. On some occasions when I have hosted meetings and invited people to offer a personal introduction, I have suggested that people describe what it is that they actually do in their workplace, rather than rely on merely saying what it is on their contract of employment.

I was always taken aback that people would disregard this opening and instead fall back on the name given to the job that they did. On some occasions, I embellished this invitation by suggesting people could share the work that they did in their role that gave them the most pleasure and motivated them the most. As with so much so-called 'facilitation' in business settings, I am now of the mind that this infantilised those with whom I was working. Moreover, it underscored the negative power dynamics that exist between the facilitator and the group. Finally, there is a strong sense that facilitation is an intermediation that allows senior leadership to abdicate their intrinsic responsibility to foster conversation and connection across corporate contexts.

In the vast majority of instances where I invited a group to share pleasure and motivation, people preferred to embrace the shorthand of a job title rather than articulate what enlivened them in terms of their role in the workplace. This may, of course, have been about simple speed of response:

DOI: 10.4324/9781003592624-2

these introductory elements of a convocation are not seen as central to the intention of the event, viewed instead as something to get past promptly in order to get to the substance of the coming together. However, it may also have been a small act of resistance to a company demand that they share something intimate about themselves.

Fresh in my mind as I write this is a conversational exchange this morning at my local shops after I had dropped my son off at school. I had walked up through the park with another parent – and, as we crossed so that I could pop to buy a newspaper, she greeted a man standing on the kerbside with a large paper carrier bag. She asked him what he was up to and his shoulders fell slightly when he said, 'I'm off to the managers' meeting.' I couldn't help myself and ended up interjecting, 'Ooooh, that sounds like fun!'

He grinned back at me and suddenly shared that, despite being in his current role for some time and having worked in retail for more than 25 years (much of it at one of the biggest names on the High Street), he still had to attend this training event designed apparently to teach him about customer service. Mindful of a LinkedIn post I had been following for a couple of days,[1] where the author had openly challenged the concept of the icebreaker, I observed that this fun day in prospect would doubtless start with an exercise such as this, perhaps homing in on a question like one of those shared in the LinkedIn post that people find particularly oppressive: 'Share a fun fact about yourself'!

The word 'fun' is doing a lot of heavy lifting in this context: it is a manifestation of the enforced jollity that is a key feature of corporate life, particularly when organisations require their workforce – or part thereof – to come together. It corrodes the membrane that quite reasonably can be said to exist between our personal and our professional lives. And the request to share in this way – which carries with it both the corporate power surrounding the event and the power of the group, in respect to those alongside whom we work – is very difficult to resist. This means that we accommodate to its intrusiveness by either actually sharing something that might ordinarily only be relevant amongst our friends and family or we confect something that feels safe for us to share in this context. Overall, then, not much fun is being had – and honesty is profoundly compromised.

Acknowledging how superficial and discomforting such opening activities can feel at a work event, I want to draw attention to the fact that this reliance on filling a gap created by a 'facilitator' with a job title can reinforce hierarchy, as job titles are often built around signifiers of positional seniority. In most instances, each tier in an organisation is smaller than the one below – and each carries with it a word or phrase such as; Manager; Head of; Assistant Director; Deputy Director; Director; and Chief something or other, up to and including Chief Executive. Our retreat into these descriptors may in some instances be a means for us to manage some anxiety about our role and what we do.

From an existentialist perspective, the job title – perhaps even the job description too, along with its associated person specification – presupposes an essence to which we should be moving. Substituting that job title for a description of how we experience our work and what we do in the course of it effaces our existence in favour of a label related to some alien notion of essence. This is an early intimation of the fact that minute by minute in an organisational context our freedom is drastically inhibited not just by the regime of control that exists therein – involving those above us and those above them dictating what it is we should do, how we should do it, and – indeed – how we should think about it – but also by the plethora of ways of being and doing that appear around us.

Free to be unfree

The focus in existentialism on the freedom that we have to live our lives is both central to its thinking and, at the same time, problematic in practice. Over the course of the eight years of paid employment I had in advance of stepping away from salaried work, I started to think at a deeply reflexive level about the work we are all expected to do in our capitalist society, how we are required to do that, and the contexts in which we find ourselves doing it. These observations were developed through the application of a critical perspective, which meant that initially I kept silent about them in corporate settings but gradually began to find the confidence to give voice to these opinions.

In terms of the seven types of silence that seem apparent in most human social circumstances – and particularly in the workplace – this could be perceived as a confluence of two of those types: it was both a silence that was *imposed* and one that was *chosen* (Cole & Higgins, 2023, pp. 4–5). This means that the freedom of which existentialism speaks is far from straightforward. Usefully, Sartre provides some thoughts as to how this tension between circumstances that demand our silence and our choice to comply with that imposition when considering the crucial notion of *thrownness*.

This concept undergirds a great deal of existentialist thinking but is openly acknowledged in the work of Heidegger and thereafter in Sartre's thought. In simple terms, it means that one moment I was not in the world; indeed, the very idea of 'I' cannot be said to have any sort of presence in real time ahead of the me that appears in the world. In an instant, I find myself in the world, having to navigate all manner of complex circumstances in a wholly unprepared way. This line of thinking is helpfully expanded upon thus:

> Man is thrown into existence, each one is thrown into his own particular existential situation. From the human point of view, it is rather like the throw of the dice. Just as you may throw a three or a six, so in life you might come up American or Vietnamese, white or black, affluent or destitute, ill-natured or good-natured, intelligent or stupid.
> (Macquarrie, 1973, p. 191)

Self-evidently, then, our freedom can only arise at the precise time that we are thrown into the world. Before that point, there is nothing in existence to exercise anything akin to freedom. We appear from nothingness and then instantly take up the challenge of navigating the immediacy of our existence moment by moment. It is here that Sartre introduces two moderating ideas that enable us to understand the world and our place in it, namely *transcendence* and *facticity*, key concepts to which I will turn my attention a little later in this chapter.

To add a little more context before that exploration, yes, we have appeared from nowhere. Crucially, we should not be thought to arrive in the world embodying a lineage from which we cannot escape. Instead, we patently arrive in a context in no way of our making that wraps around us in a 360 fashion: the past sits behind us, unconnected to our life but potentially giving it shape, depending on how we choose to acknowledge and understand it; the future is wholly unwritten other than the crucial recognition – from the perspective of what is called *temporality* – that there is a finitude to our lives, although we are free to shape that presence from the moment we embrace our agency; and the present is the place where we engage with our existence, in respect to acting in the world, which in turn defines who it is that we are.

Inclusive freedom

There are clearly implications arising out of this view of the world in respect to working towards a genuinely inclusive workplace. The dominant ideological perspective that can be seen to shape discussions in respect to this topic tend towards an essentialist perspective, wherein politically crafted and crudely generalised notions of whiteness and blackness are seen to define us as individuals whilst we try to make our way through our lives. Such an overview leaves the person being identified not by their acts in the course of their existence but by some historical context which they never actually inhabited.

To an extent, then, this determinism resonates with the religious notion of the doctrine of Original Sin (DOS). This derives not so much from the gospels as from subsequent exegesis by Christian thinkers and authorities – and has its origin in interpretations of the fall of Adam and Eve, an event which appears in the first book of the Old Testament (Quinn, 2010). It is argued that the foundations of DOS as understood across the range of Christian perspectives can be summarised thus:

> (S0) All human beings (except, at most, four) suffer from a kind of corruption that makes it very likely that they will fall into sin.
>
> Many (perhaps most) go on to affirm the following two claims as well
>
> (S1) All human beings (except, at most, four) suffer from a kind of corruption that makes in inevitable that they will fall into sin, and this corruption is a consequence of the first sin of the first man.
>
> (S2) All human beings (except, at most, four) are guilty from birth in the eyes of God, and this guilt is a consequence of the first sin of the first man.
>
> (Rea, 2007, p. 319)

Having identified these underpinnings of the DOS, it is intimated that its function extends beyond the theological into an altogether more secular realm. Specifically, it is suggested that it offers an *ex post facto* rationalisation for the prevalence of sin in the world (Rea, 2007, p. 320). As someone who spent his 20s immersed in socialist politics and Marxist thought, this declaration seems to mirror the ways in which my comrades and I would rationalise the failure of the working class to be the agents of the socio-economic change that Marx asserted was scientifically certain to occur. A reminder, then, that faith – an oftentimes unthinking and wholly unchallenged adherence to a credo, which in turn dominates your agency throughout the time that you are wedded to it – is not the sole preserve of religion but is a facet of all Grand Narratives (Lyotard, 1984). In these framings, the underpinning view of the world is left largely unchallenged and predictions arising from that view are taken to be certainties.

Beyond rationalising the fact of sin in the world, DOS is also seen to be a justification for the fact that even the newborn baby requires a saviour, so needs to be drawn into membership of the Church at the very earliest opportunity. Here we can discern the way in which religious thought and practice pivots around the notions of essence; in this instance, the very essence of a human being is taken to be that – without once acting in the world – they are in the midst of sin and so need to atone for something that precedes them.

As a Christian writer and one of the first existentialists, Soren Kierkegaard is said to posit an alternative perspective in this regard. In an exposition around the relationship between the fall, in which Adam commits the first sin, and what Kierkegaard calls hereditary sin, he asserts that there is a faulty logic, wherein Adam's sin is acknowledged as a consequence while the first sins of others are a sign of a state of sinfulness. Overall, he concludes that there is no basis for the idea of Original Sin (Kierkegaard, 1980). In this view of the theology, there is no meaningful connection between the two, which provides a foundation for the notion of thrownness, based on the assertion that we arrive in the world unsullied by that which occurred in that place before us.

Some take an alternative perspective to this, honing in on the specific issue of being thrown into living as a person of colour – and focusing in on having to exercise one's freedom and choice in a social context in light of that. In analysing this distinctive approach to the challenges of human existence, it is argued that:

> From a humanistic perspective, Black existentialism is the lens through which one can begin to see where inequity, racialization, and marginalization are situated as Black people search to experience agency in the world. This is because Black existentialism has roots in advocacy, social justice, and radicalism as major tenets.
>
> (Vereen et al., 2017, p. 73)

It is also argued that this philosophical approach has expanded out of an intersection between philosophies of existence derived from both the African and African-Caribbean traditions of seeing and engaging with the world and also existentialism at large (Henry, 1997). Importantly, Black existentialism – drawing those two strands together intellectually – is said to offer the following critical conclusion: '[O]ppression may be seen as an existential violation, an ontological crime … [It] robs people of their identity as surely as exploitation robs people of the fruits of their labour. Oppression imposes rigid, stultifying identities on its victims' (Birt, 1997, p. 206).

The author goes on to acknowledge that oppression is not the exclusive preserve of people of colour, particularly in the type of global socio-economic systems that we all presently inhabit – and look set to do so for some time. Indeed, he concludes that most of humanity endures oppression to some degree, when one factors in variables of both class and gender (Birt, 1997, p. 207). It is also possible to argue persuasively from an existentialist position that oppression is implicit in being a human being, because – whilst we are granted freedom – the complexity of navigating existence means that this is constantly under pressure.

Perhaps more importantly, some people have argued that the focus on a predominantly racialized engagement with the idea of existence can be seen to draw upon precisely the sort of essentialism which existentialism explicitly rejects. This position is strongly expressed by what one author deigns to define as a new intelligentsia, who are seeking to challenge the accepted precepts of what gets called 'wokeness' in popular parlance across our societies (Ungar-Sargon, 2020). One of those said to be part of this nascent movement is Chloe Valdary, who is cited in the piece as follows: '"Racial essentialism is very reductive and actually oppressive", Valdary told me. "Ironically, it reduces us as individuals to our immutable characteristics, which is precisely what we were supposed to be fighting against"' (Ungar-Sargon, 2020).

It is precisely essentialism of this sort that can be seen to undergird racism around the world, as from within this view it is taken to be the case that many aspects of race and ethnicity are in some way natural, unavoidable and hence largely immutable, potentially leading to the observation that, on the basis of their race, 'an individual is fundamentally a certain sort of person' (Verkuyten, 2003, p. 371). Moreover, some research suggests that essentialism actively promotes prejudice – even, it is suggested, among those who may be part of the group that an essentialist view denigrates – and does so in terms of the reification of social hierarchy (Mandalaywala et al., 2018).

On a commercial website called Theory of Enchantment that arises from the work of Chloe Valdary, the point is made that supremacy is based on the notion that there are some people who we deem to be below us – and that we all of us at some point feel superior to another. This chimes with a view of the world that is often referred to as *rankism*, wherein the world can be seen to be populated by two categories, the *somebodies* and the *nobodies* (Fuller, 2004). Rankism inveigles itself into all manner of social dynamics, including issues of class, gender, disability, and race. However, it also stands alone and manifests itself in any circumstances wherein people find themselves in relationship with others. The Theory of Enchantment site goes on to argue that:

> Supremacy's roots lie in psychological insecurity. Psychological insecurity is pervasive, which explains why many current approaches to fighting supremacy are themselves supremacist. For example,

> in attempting to fight racism, many approaches traffic in racial essentialism – the belief that the essential, most important characteristic about a human being is the category of race to which they belong. This encourages and even rewards participants for caricaturing, prejudging, and disparaging others on the basis of race. This accelerates a rhetorical arms race, which defines the culture war today, and explains why we often feel that race relations are getting worse, not better.
>
> (Theory of Enchantment, 2024)

All of which reinforces the potential vitality, even liberational potential, that comes with stepping into freedom and the making of choice in a world that we could not possibly have chosen to suddenly find ourselves thrown into. It leaves me all the more aware of the implications and wider effects of how I opt to live my life moment by moment – and the curious way in which I am patently at liberty as a free agent to embrace any action that might feel personally and ethically appropriate to me, while the unchosen circumstances of life defines in the finest detail how I might think about those options.

Being thrown means you have to land somewhere

I am acutely aware of the limits that exist on my freedom, notwithstanding the existentialist focus on the centrality of that liberty. As is the case for many of us, I can look back on instances in my life where my inaction was actually an action and – as a result – obviously had an impact. In other situations, I have actively and explicitly made a choice even though – in my heart of hearts – I knew that I was not acting authentically, but choosing to comply with the choices of others, and disappearing the choice that would have been the one I would have made if I'd embraced my own agency and freedom.

Equally, I can think of times where I made a choice in good faith. I vividly recall deputising for my boss one day and attending a meeting for the senior leaders in the company. Disconcertingly, it was a session where that upper cadre of management were to spend time with a new CEO. I sat in this space feeling deeply uncomfortable, constantly haunted by the thought that I was where I should not be. This negativity arose despite my general scepticism about the current corporate hierarchy: it seemed deeply contradictory that I could both reject and comply with a top-down structure like this.

I have since reflected on the situation and come up with two possible explanations for the way I experienced that meeting. Firstly, in broad terms, this environment felt completely alien to me, a circumstance that ordinarily I did as much as I possibly could to distance myself from. But alongside this was a general sense that it was a performative gathering whence nothing of real value could emerge. Thinking of it in those theatrical terms reinforced for me the fact that I was an understudy – and one that wasn't fully acquainted with my part or the setting of the drama that was unfolding … and didn't rate at all the play in which I found myself performing.

All of this was reinforced by the group dynamics of the gathering. It was easy to discern powerful tensions between the new CEO and the person that they were replacing as they sat awkwardly in close proximity in that meeting room. It was also apparent in the withdrawn nature of the other senior leaders in the room, most of whom – in keeping with the behaviours one tends to see at senior levels of organisations – would ordinarily be the people in the room who spoke the most and often spoke the loudest. As an aside, this is in keeping with the *babble hypothesis*, which suggests that the gobshite is normally socially identified as the leader – or the person most likely to step into leadership at some point (MacLaren et al., 2020).

Back to the meeting in question. Following an artificially positive preamble, wherein all assembled – including, of course, me – maintained a veneer of civility and respect, despite the negative dynamics that undergirded the gathering, the new CEO broke cover and asked how people were feeling in light of significant corporate change, not least the crucial change at the top that this gathering manifested. I had spoken to many in the space prior to this meeting, so was extremely aware of how angry and anxious people were in the room. But they opted to play by the rules of the company game, affecting a positive expression and opting for silence.

I recall in that moment thinking that I would give voice to my feelings about the circumstances as honestly as I could … and suddenly I found my hand slightly raised and my observations echoing ominously around the room. Interestingly, the new CEO opted not to look at me as I spoke, instead choosing to type away on the iPad that they had propped in front of them, a fortification that allowed them to retreat into their leadership castle, whose walls I could not scale. Their furtive notetaking appeared to signify engagement but for me there was a complete disconnect between my speaking and their typing. Their actions were designed to suggest that they were avidly capturing what it was that I was saying, although transcription like this is not at all the same as listening to hear, hearing to understand, and understanding to create space for dialogue (Cole & Higgins, 2023). Far from it; it offered the illusion of engagement, whilst allowing the leader to absent themselves from the intensity of what was being said.

This instance provides insight into the existentialist notions of good and bad faith or authenticity and inauthenticity, which is intimately related to the freedom that we are deemed to be able to exercise and find ourselves either acting on or not, and what happens in a world where good and bad faith encounter each other. This leads to the important observation that:

> The lowliest and the highest of us all possess the power and the importance that is given to us merely through the insight that we are born free and that nothing can change this fact ... [T]he understanding of free will gives us a sense of supreme accountability: the willingness to accept responsibility and blame for all of our acts is a central ingredient in an authentic existence.
>
> (Block & Koestenbaum, 2023, p. 17)

Freedom and its limits

I arrived in the world unsullied by the history that preceded me and in which I played no part because nothing of me could reasonably be said to exist across the millennia before I was thrown into the world. Thereafter, I was not merely present ... but have had to actively navigate that presence in light of the fact that I was now responsible for my choices in that context. Sartre's interpretation of existence considering this circumstance that we all face is said to be as follows:

> It is first and foremost defined by my acts and in my acts ... You are nothing other than your life, says a character in one of Sartre's plays. You define yourself by your acts ... Man is at first a project lived subjectively; he chooses what he will be, and he will be what he has chosen to be.
>
> (Wahl, 1959/2019, p. 38)

Borrowing from Heidegger, this is where Sartre usefully introduces ideas of *transcendence* and *facticity*. Apologies here for the philosophical jargon: as noted earlier at the start of this book, I have tried twice to read Heidegger's *Being and Time* but, on both occasions, barely got beyond the introduction. Partly, it's the richness of the thinking being articulated, albeit by a decidedly flawed individual who aligned himself with the Nazis and never publicly came to terms with that affiliation when the Second World War ended. Partly, it's the translation from the German and the author's use of a variety of neologisms. And, partly, it's just a level of impenetrability in terms of the writing itself, which does little to encourage accessibility for the general reader.

In terms of offering a somewhat clearer and grounded definition of these two ideas, I would say this: my awareness of – and engagement with – my own freedom to choose in the world and to shape my life through the act of choosing is central to existentialist thought. And, while the world that came before the moment I was thrown into it cannot be said to be integral to me and my life, it remains the case that I am compelled to navigate my existence in circumstances where I am surrounded by others and where the practicalities of the world in which I have found myself both facilitate and constrain my capacity for choice and the choices available to me. My freedom allows me to transcend, but facticity places limits on that transcendent liberty.

Even taking into account the interrelation between my agency and the context in which I find myself, existentialism argues that my freedom remains limitless, which seems a paradoxical assertion. However, this offers us insight into what is meant by the freedom that we have – and the way in which we might act in bad faith to deny it. Let me use a personal example to try and illustrate this.

Around 20 years ago, I was diagnosed with something called a spasmodic dysphonia, a condition that means that I struggle to get my vocal chords to do what I want them to do. It is a neurological complaint, wherein sometimes, when I need it to be closed, my voice box is open – and vice versa. More recently, the condition has seemingly worsened, which means that my voice is constantly impaired these days … and occasionally it barely functions, especially on those occasions when I have used it a great deal in terms of having a number of meetings back-to-back or running a longish workshop or teaching session.

The only possible treatment is a botox injection directly into my larynx. I had this done on one occasion a while after the diagnosis, but – whereas presently I can just about force my voice out, albeit with a great deal of effort and knowing its quality will be poor – the treatment reduced my voice to a whisper, which could not be heard at all in noisy environments, such as a pub. It was a formative experience for me, I now realise, to be sat alongside a group of friends in a bustling bar yet forced to be silent … and, instead, have to listen to the conversation in the role of a bystander.

I do not have freedom in regard to this disabling condition: it is something that I have to accept as inescapable. I do not have the choice of not having the condition, which is a fine example of facticity in my existence. Sartre writes about the impact disability has on transcendence at some length, leading one commentator to helpfully summarise how transcendence and facticity interrelate:

> Even if a person is disabled and unable to walk, … his freedom is unlimited. He is not free to walk in the sense of being at liberty to walk, but he is still free to choose the meaning of his disability and hence responsible for his response to it … If a disabled person considers his disability the ruination of his life then that is a choice he has made for which he alone is responsible. He is free to choose his disability positively. To strive, for example, to be a successful para-athlete or to spend the time he used to spend playing football writing a book or fundraising.
>
> (Cox, 2011, p. 49)

This reminds me of a conversation I had with a ward manager in the NHS hospital in which I was working many years back. We were discussing how the notion of 'customer service' sat somewhat uncomfortably when considering the delivery of health care. They offered the following observation: there are instances on a busy medical ward where it is necessary for a patient to move. A member of the nursing might usher them away from their bed and walk them into the day room. But, at that point, you can offer choice, asking the patient – for example – whether they would prefer to sit and watch the TV or look out of the window into the grounds.

Work and facticity

The circumstances into which we are thrown are not at all of our making and have to be thoughtfully navigated. Intriguingly, we have to acknowledge this facticity in the course of our existence in two ways: firstly, we have to recognise that the situation in which we literally 'find ourselves' is constantly shifting. For example, I recall a family story that I heard once or twice that intimated that my maternal grandfather had lied about his age in order to enlist as a young man to fight in the First World War. Recently, as I tried to explore details from that side of the family via Google, documents came to light that seemingly referred to Grandad – but suggested that he had actively applied to be exempted from being called up, because of his crucial role as a wage earner in his family at that time.

Insofar as my mother passed away some years ago and my father followed some years later, I was struck that – while archives might exist that could offer insight into what actually happened then – the voices to whom I would ordinarily turn to clarify something like this are no longer there, so the facticity that perhaps felt certain earlier in my life now feels decidedly frayed and lacking a grounding in reality.

While the facticity specific to us as individuals erodes over the course of our lives, it must also surely be the case that our efforts at transcendence serve to weave a fresh facticity into which others will be thrown in the future. To an extent, this is a reminder that whilst we are the product of our choices, the things that we choose have the effect of shaping the situation in which we – and crucially many others – live.

For example, for someone assuming the role of a senior corporate leader, it is critical to bear in mind that – despite the myriad textbooks and 'thought leadership' that suggest the contrary – there is no essential definition of leadership to which that person can aspire. Instead, their existence in the role of leader and the choices that they make are what shapes and guides their presence in life as a leader … and, at the same time, contributes to a far bigger picture, namely how we might best understand leadership by developing a rich awareness of what people do and how they do it when assuming that role of leader.

Applying the ideas of existentialism to the contemporary practice of leadership in corporate contexts, I am moved to observe the tension between essence and existence. So much of our leadership thinking in and around the business world is shaped and bounded by the idea that we can isolate critical attitudes, aptitudes, and activities that are then said to make up leadership. These are then used to measure competence and also shape the syllabus for leadership development. The most recent report into NHS leadership undertaken by a retired general is so distorted by this essentialist approach as to render it meaningless in the field of practice (Messenger, 2022). Instead, an existentialist approach beneficially allows the following to occur:

> [I]f there is no essence of leadership, leaders and other members are free to exercise freedom as they wish or to construct leadership relationships with those around them as best suits them and their circumstances. Any definitions of leadership or itemizations of leadership characteristics become themselves constrictions, excluding, as they do, other personal and interpersonal dimensions, from consideration in any analysis.
>
> (Lawler, 2005, p. 227)

This resonates with some of the experiences people in the NHS had as they faced the sheer novelty of the Covid-19 pandemic … and were suddenly confronted with a situation that was uncertain and unknowable. In a major research exercise into the experience of NHS staff in the course of the pandemic, in which I was involved, the following insights emerged into how the crisis both adversely impacted traditional leadership while also allowing a different form of leadership to emerge through dispersed freedom, responsibility, and choice:

> Many participants described examples of what can be considered transformative and adaptive leadership in action through the urgent pressures of the pandemic, through necessity, working across organisational boundaries, using initiative without guidelines. For example, 'we have pulled out of the bag completely different models of care', such as outreach work for vaccinations, creating online materials for staff retention.
>
> (Bristol Leadership and Change Centre – UWE Bristol, 2021, p. 28)

The disruption brought about by the pandemic – an event which had a clear sense of the existential to it – has led some to consider its positive impact on leadership in corporate settings in the longer term. For example, some discussed how reactions to the crisis evidenced what the German revolutionary Rosa Luxemburg called eminent leadership, an adaptive practice, which stands in sharp contrast to the sterility and immobility of traditional models of leading (Witzel, 2022, p. 131).

It is suggested that these leaders had capabilities suited to the specific circumstances, alongside the capacity to act as a conduit so that information could pass unhindered across the systems of which they were part. Additionally, they were willing to step forward into leadership and, in doing so, discovered that people were actively willing to follow them, whereas traditional leadership merely assumes a followership that arises out of the relationship expressed in formal hierarchy. They eschewed the standard instruments of managerialism, namely reward and coercion, because they were not a formal part of the administrative infrastructure but created change through the influence that their presence and the respect that they commanded provided to them (Witzel, 2022, p. 131).

Dividing the world into two uneven categories, with leaders being the dominant yet smaller of the two, while followers – definitely the predominant group – are broadly seen as passive, is a crudely essentialist exercise. Allowing this binary to persist unchallenged in our workplaces denies us the simple fact of the freedom and choice that is a key feature of our existence. Additionally, it presupposes a definition of leader that is largely built out of the people who have presently found their way into such positions, thereby generating a crude circularity where the system endlessly reproduces itself.

Freedom to be what we choose to be at work

I invited people via LinkedIn to reflect on five questions that related to an existentialist perspective on living our lives in the workplace. The first inquired into the extent to which people felt free to live their lives on their own terms in the context of their work. The following comments arose out of this particular inquiry into workplace freedom, and to my mind offer powerful insight into the constraining quality of workplace processes, culture, and relationships:

a. 'I experience all sorts of constraints mainly linked to other's desires of what I will and won't do and my own anxieties … and around risks to my income and reputation … Ultimately from an existential perspective these moments come down to choice and authenticity of bad faith in Sartre's view.'
b. 'I have found an implicit trade-off of sacrificing freedom for organisational goals to work reasonably well for me.'
c. 'I have recently left … because of a lack of freedom. Individual freedom wasn't policed per se – individuals were implicitly free to do (or not) whatever they pleased. The problem was more that individuals were not given the agency to help the organisation achieve its goals. Being dragged down into a swamp of bureaucratic mediocrity was a painful experience as I had invested so much of my identity with the organisation over decades.'
d. 'In my life in organisations I found that my hardest moments came when I felt oppressed by people using hierarchy to force home a world view. Freedom in that case often felt like the freedom to choose to leave. Of course there was plenty of freedom to act, believe and stay true to what felt right in most day to day work.'
e. 'I left … after 22 years to work independently. Now I feel a greater sense of freedom than before. I think my work experience … was very parent/child, constrained, and there was not the freedom to express myself fully or offer my expertise for fear of consequences and the wider anxiety of being rejected by the group.'

f. 'I've changed direction, role, sector, and found that freedom. Or [however] rightly or wrongly phrased I feel I have permission to practice [that freedom]. I've noticed that although I have this [freedom], and I am my own instrument I look for sounding boards sense checking my reading of the Organisation as if I don't trust myself.'
g. 'I am fortunate to live in an organisation where freedom of expression is permitted and I have a degree of autonomy in my work. This provides scope to pursue activities that are of interest to myself, as long as they are aligned with the organisation's overall values and objectives. This gives greater flexibility in achieving my own personal ambitions.'
h. 'My sense of freedom probably lasted [for a] few minutes whenever I had it. That feeling might have been mixed with a sense of content, satisfaction, rise of initiative and simply good mood. But overall, in the culture of intolerance to mistakes [I am in,] I tend to feel limited [and] that caused a lot of anxiety and fear which led to stopping believing in myself.'
i. 'I work remotely and have a high degree of autonomy so to a degree I have a great deal of freedom to work/live on my own terms. The role I do and the expectations I place upon myself though have their own consequences though.'
j. 'I'm not sure if we can ever experience complete freedom. There are always choices to be made. I might enjoy the freedom to do the work I love and at the same time be working for a critical/harsh/controlling manager. And there are different dimensions to freedom. Freedom to do the work we enjoy, freedom to earn money to pay the mortgage. And our conceptualisation of freedom is contextualised within our past experiences and vicarious learning. Freedom is linked to what is important to us. I remember feeling trapped in a job I hated when I was in my 20s. Trapped by not being able to resign because I had to pay the rent. Trapped because the job was well paid and it enabled me to enjoy expensive hobbies. Of course I could have resigned and gone back to live with my mum but this was an undesirable choice.'

These observations immediately reminded me of my own experience back in July 2023. After nigh on 40 years in salaried jobs and seven years in my then current position, the overall organisation in which I found myself allegedly took instruction from a large management consultancy that they needed to downsize by 40 per cent. Importantly, I had never applied to actually work there, nor would I ever have done, given my view that it cost an inordinate amount of tax-pounds and yet offered little by way of value for money. As is so often the case, I had landed there in light of merger and acquisition decisions in which I played no part.

I could have chosen to leave, of course, but I so adored the work I was doing that I chose to turn a blind eye to how we were being arbitrarily moved from one host corporation to another. This is a reminder of the argument that there is a tripartite of closely interconnected possibilities of response that consumers, members of a firm or social organisation, can make in response to any dissatisfaction they experience. These three being to exit, to give voice, or to show loyalty through word, act, or deed. It is suggested that 'To resort to voice, rather than exit, is for the customer or member to make an attempt at changing the practices, policies, and outputs of the firm from which one buys or of the organization to which one belongs' (Hirschman, 1970, p. 30). Voice might be chosen by an individual 'either as a complement to exit or as a substitute for it' (Hirschman, 1970, p. 30).

A key reason why I eschewed exit and voice (and offered a simulation of loyalty) was that, after so many years in the workplace, I had finally discovered that work could be something more than an experience to endure to obtain reward but was actually something positive from which I derived meaning and a personal sense of deep satisfaction. Around me, of course, I was mindful of the managerial manoeuvres, where the term 'consultation' was used and abused in the HR sense of meaning that I was being told by the people 'upstairs' what was going to happen. The consultation exercise was shrouded in the pretence that if I offered any commentary in response to their plans for me and the others in this place, it would be taken seriously and used to create a revised version of the plan.

The only comments that can be incorporated in this way are ones that raise an issue which can be accommodated without disturbing the overall intention of the change exercise. In existentialist terms, I was free to write back to the HR department to say that I was unconvinced by the seemingly arbitrary figure of a 40 per cent downsizing in staff numbers. I have no doubt that if I had spoken up, I'd have received some desiccated corporate response, thanking me for taking time to raise this issue. The only managerial response would likely have been to double down on the messaging to try to convince everyone – including me – that there was some compelling logic behind it.

This serves to remind us of the complex tension that exists between transcendence – living our lives with a degree of awareness and a recognition that we are free to choose how we experience that existence – and that notion of facticity, meaning the context and constraints within which we are able to exercise that freedom. This requires us to be reflexively aware of those times where our failure to choose in the course of our lives is, in itself, a choice. Kierkegaard offers insight into the profound difficulty of being free in circumstances that limit that freedom when he explores two competing perspectives on the world and seems to encourage us to interrogate these approaches through the notion of needing to choose (Kierkegaard, 1843/1992).

In regard to this defining element of human existence, De Beauvoir draws the powerful conclusion that 'Ethics is the triumph of freedom over facticity' (De Beauvoir, 1947/2018, p. 48), which resonates very much with the idea of speaking up. By making this connection, it reinforces the idea that the choice to give voice is a fundamentally existentialist action – and that choosing to say something aloud is an intrinsically ethical act. This resonates with the assertion that 'there is a concrete bond between freedom and existence; to will man free is to will there to *be* being, it is to will the disclosure of being in the joy of existence' (De Beauvoir, 1947/2018, p. 146) [Emphasis in original].

To humanise the workplace, we need to consider two actions arising from this existentialist analysis. Firstly, at a personal level, I have to acknowledge the freedom that I have – while, at the same time, recognising that I am constantly facing the need to make choices, oftentimes in a context where my options will be constrained by the circumstances in which I seek to live my temporally bounded life. The latter gives an added urgency to seizing the day and engaging with the world in a way that allows me to embrace my agency. It also brings to the fore the important observation that

> bad faith is more like an ongoing project of *self-distraction* or *self-evasion* than self-deception … [B]ad faith is not an abstract concept but a concrete existential phenomenon – the attitude, disposition and way of behaving of real people in real situations..
>
> (Cox, 2011, p. 59)

Secondly, I am also responsible for choosing to create the circumstances wherein those around me are also able to exercise their freedom and choice. This applies to me as an individual or as a member of a community of others. Equally, it is particularly important in terms of people practising corporate leadership, in terms of doing so by embracing existentialism. That connection is envisaged by some as being generated by the idea of authenticity, which has contrasting definitional notions in corporate settings, the first of which is essentialist and suggests that people should allow their true self to appear in the role – whereas the second is existentialist, which contests the very notion that a true self (or a role model in a given area of activity) exists (Lawler & Ashman, 2012).

To embrace these ways of being is to acknowledge our responsibilities as a human being, defining ourselves in the course of our existence through our deeds. We are advised by this that:

> existence is becoming. Passion and decision are movements. Existence is not definable, but by calling it a movement, a becoming, we characterise it legitimately, for we define it in terms of something that is itself undefinable. Existence is temporality, continuous becoming, a task.
>
> (Wahl, 1959/2019, p. 31)

And we need to immerse ourselves in that telling of the story of our lives, so as to embrace an ethical stance that does not rely on an external framework but arises out of our being in the world.

I spoke earlier about people's tendency to retreat behind their job titles from the discomforting and dreary experience of a company awayday. These labels represent just one essentialist function among many, with others being *inter alia* consumer, producer, and citizen. A person deludes themselves by stepping in and out of these and other positions in a way that means that 'The rather horrible expression time table perfectly describes his life' (Marcel, 2018, p. 7). Stepping away from the tags that we place on ourselves – or others place on us – frees up space and time for us to embrace the freedom with which we are imbued once thrown into world … and two crucial names in that sense are *leader* and *follower*.

What are the voices speaking about freedom telling me?

Limits and liberty

When I read about people's experience of freedom and choice at work, I was struck by how the facticity of our corporate existence tends to derive from two sources. Firstly, there is the expectation of others, both those who sit above us in the corporate pecking order and those with whom we collaborate around us. As you can see from the comments shared above, one person speaks about the experience of being constrained by the desires of others. This is a reminder that we can often feel that we are at the whim of those with whom we come together in the workplace.

The interconnections between people should not be thought of as founded on rationality, even though organisational structure often tacitly claims that as its undergirding. Instead, we need to focus on the fact that we are all turning up in a corporate space as human agents, which means that our individual efforts at transcendence will knock against those of the people around us. Another respondent speaks about feeling oppressed by those who utilise their position in a hierarchy to promote their particular perspective. This powerfully reminds us of the interplay between our freedom and the context in which we are looking to exercise it.

By the same token, the discursive counterpoint these days to that traditional perspective on organisational life which can be seen to rely upon rationalism is the idea that 'We're all in this together' (Cole & Higgins, 2022, pp. 138–144), an artificial flattening of the workplace relations that can be argued to create an illusion of even greater freedom and choice. Even those workplaces that assert their flatness remain filled with people who – as several commented – find their agency limited by anguish that arises out of their presence as a person in this context. There is a reference to cultures of intolerance, fear of consequences, and anxiety around social rejection: these are things that – notwithstanding the stated nature of the workplace in which we find ourselves – will spring up in the course of our existence and lead us into bad faith.

As we have seen earlier, this complex notion is one wherein we are mindful of the context in which we find ourselves and yet knowingly make decisions and take positions that run counter to what we know. It is often erroneously thought that bad faith can be seen as self-deception, but the deceiving takes place openly and honestly. It means that 'the duality of the deceiver and the deceived does not exist here. Bad faith on the contrary implies in essence the unity of a single consciousness' (Sartre, 1965/1993, p. 150). In keeping with the analysis of a waiter – who has embraced the artificiality of 'waiter-ness' so comprehensively that their presence as a free and choosing human being has been drastically impaired – absorption into a role allows us to evade the expectation that we should make decisions and act freely in the world (Sartre, 1943/1957, pp. 59–60).

Waiting and leading

The example used in this seminal work is a waiter, which is a very distinctive occupation in terms of behavioural expectations, alongside defined activities and attitudes. But other jobs can be framed in this existential way, an observation that compels us to acknowledge that – in terms of being a manager or leader in the contemporary workforce – those roles are also defined by outlook and action in a working context. In simple terms, 'The waiter, we might think, is just doing his job. But Sartre's point here is that we must be careful not to collapse our boundless existential potential into things like our jobs' (Maden, 2023).

This is particularly the case with those who occupy the role of leader: what needs to be done by a person in this position is wrapped up in indicators of their position derived from topics such as stance and presence, how they speak to others, and an expectation of decisiveness. Those who slide into these positions without recognition of their humanity are living in bad faith. This is particularly ironic insofar as such people are seen to be decisive, directive, and focused … but they are hiding their existence behind an essentialist notion that paradoxically banishes their freedom.

Assuming that there is a definition of a role to which we should then aspire denies the simple fact that we are in the world as an individual (albeit one closely connected to others) and need to find our own way in that context, a situation that finds us facing a new choice more or less constantly as we live our lives in the unfurling present. Here it is useful to consider Heidegger's notions of *Sein* and *Dasein*, where the latter 'is a being that does not simply occur among other beings. Rather it is ontically distinguished by the fact that in its Being this being is concerned *about* its very being' (Heidegger, 1993, p. 53) [Emphasis in original].

Elsewhere, mirroring this distinction, Sartre speaks of being-in-itself and being-for-itself. In his novel entitled *Nausea*, he offers a fictional account of a person coming to terms with having agency in the world – and being different to an object such as a tree trunk or a piece of furniture. The distinction between these two states is usefully explicated as follows:

> Because the for-itself (like man) lacks a predetermined essence, it must create itself from nothingness. Nothingness, according to Sartre, is the defining characteristic of the for-itself. A tree is a tree and has no ability to change or create its own existence. Man, on the other hand, creates himself through his actions in the world. Man, as an object-for-itself, must actuate his own being rather than simply being, as the object-in-itself does.
>
> (Admin, 2023)

Turning up in the day-to-day

The focus here on leadership is important because of the way in which it is fetishized in contemporary business. It is also extremely illustrative of the complicated issues of freedom and choice at work. But it is not exclusive, because all that has been said thus far in respect to leadership applies equally to all of us in our organisations, regardless of the essentialist roles behind which we find ourselves sheltering. On one occasion, as the NHS trust of which I was part was forced to merge with two other organisations, three of us found ourselves competing for the same job; the coming together meant that three 'Head of' positions had been reduced to one, for which three of us in post prior to the merger were expected to apply.

I knew that I didn't want the job, partly because it was set to be all the more bureaucratised and less practice focused now that the organisation was scaling up – and primarily because I knew deep down that I would not be any good at it … so would be putting myself in harm's way. Unthinkingly, I did no preparation whatsoever for the interview: yet, although I didn't admit this to myself, I knew that I would be asked questions about the emergent new organisation. Rather, I knew I would be quizzed about the dull managerial documents that were in circulation in light of the changes being proposed. But I could find no motivation to pick them up, let alone read them. As a result, the interview was an excruciating experience and unsurprisingly I was unsuccessful in my application.

The upshot of this was that another of the three of us achieved the promotion – and I was downgraded by one pay band, albeit on a significant period of protected pay. The most profound effect on me was the loss of the Head of status that I had enjoyed for the best part of five years. I was now to be organisationally defined as an 'L&D Business Partner'. In focusing on these definitional terms, I was living in bad faith, ignoring my need to take control of how to live my life as a person confronted by choice. I had allowed the process to roll over me without taking control of my thinking about and orientation towards it. Dropping into a business partner role was meaningless; abdicating my individual responsibility to exercise my freedom was substantially more important.

This is because, as we have discussed earlier,

> Man's nature is not "fixed" as a stone's or a tree's is; he is a creature with the ability to choose, and decides what he shall become … Because he is capable of existing as a subject, a self-determining agent, man is authentic only if he exercises his potentiality. If he prefers the relative easiness and security of existing as an object (as the waiter did who disavowed his true self for that of a waiter), he is inauthentic.
>
> (Killinger, 1961, p. 304)

Structure of oppression

The second element of facticity that might be said to constrain our freedom at work is structure, as stated by several of the respondents. Here it was possible to hear how the processes, procedures, and practices that surround us – alongside all of the other organisational artefacts that define the ways in which things are expected to be done in a given context – sucked people down into a disempowering morass. This felt as if it ran strongly counter to the way in which someone had invested their identity in that corporate setting.

In my personal experience, I was especially mindful towards the end of my 40-year tenure in the salariat that the documentary framework that forms a company infrastructure has a life of its own, and that each component cannot realistically be attributed to a single author or group of authors. Indeed, a corporate document challenges the very notion of authorship, given the way in which it tends to creep back and forth across the bureaucracy, accreting fresh meaning and changed orientation every step of the way. This is why, when I work with John Higgins in terms of encouraging people to embrace criticality, reflexivity, and their ethical self, we advance an approach to Derridean deconstruction as a way of reading those documents and materials – and allow them to unravel in front of one's eyes, in light of setting aside the assumptions and presumptions that one brings to that particular item (Jones, 2003).

Someone else spoke of living in a corporate context of intolerance in regard to the making of mistakes. Certainly, the relationship that humankind has with error is far from straightforward. Attempts have been made to define and taxonomise human error, starting from the point that it always arises from some form of deviation. An argument is advanced that 'Such deviations could be from the upright (trip or stumble); from the current intention (slip or lapse); from an appropriate route towards some goal (mistake); or, in some circles, it could even involve straying from the path of righteousness (sin).' (Reason, 2008, p. 29). More importantly, it is philosophically argued that our progress in terms of human knowledge cannot be separated from the making of errors (Roberts, 2011).

Once again, we can see how the corporate life into which we are thrown idolises perfection, even if there is a lack of clarity as to what that means and what perfection might actually look like. Perfection becomes akin to the carrot, just out of reach yet constantly dangled in front of the donkey. In the workplace, we plod after it without questioning what it is that we're pursuing and neglecting the fact that we are unlikely ever to reach that particular carrot. But whilst the donkey recognises the carrot and follows it on the basis of that knowledge, lost in a routine built around the idea that this time might be the time that the beast of burden finally catches up with it, hordes of us in corporate environments are trudging behind something that is completely obscure and largely unexperienced by us.

To own these feelings in order to demonstrate the implications, I have spent many years of my working life imagining that I can deliver a solution to a business challenge that is so exquisitely designed as to be an ideal response. However, in allowing myself to get locked into that train of thought and that line of practice, I am actively effacing the positives that might well arise simply out of my presence in the world and the myriad choices that I am compelled to make in light of my freedom. Some of those choices will be ones that are far from successful … but I cannot understand success unless I stop staring into an illusory future and instead take time to look at how my decisions pan out in practice in the present.

From autonomy to autogestion

Some people who responded to the survey spoke positively about the level of autonomy that they enjoyed in their work. This resonates with scholarly work that explores topics such as job satisfaction and job design, with autonomy being a key job characteristic in terms of creating a sense of satisfaction that, in turn, can be seen to link to issues of productivity (Saragih, 2011). At a time when HR departments and other functions of managerialism are making provision of standalone initiatives that are promoted as supporting the health and well-being of their workforces, it is wise to recall that research findings suggest 'that job complexity and job autonomy significantly interacted to predict job satisfaction, turnover intentions, and psychological well-being' (Chung-Yan, 2010, p. 244).

So, if one matches complexity of work with a decent level of autonomy for the employee, one sees positive outlooks and outcomes at work. It would therefore seem that actively embracing existentialist freedom and choice has huge beneficial potential.

To move beyond the constraints of neo-liberalism, where the individual is paramount and the idea of the collective is invoked as something negative, it is worth shifting the perspective from one where we focus solely on the single person and their specific embrace of liberty in terms of thought and action to the idea of a collaboration of individuals. In this collaborative ensemble, each individual is making an initial choice to combine with others in order to create an existential collective, where autonomous beings are coming together in a way that supports the emergence in organisations of *autogestion*.

The French theorist Henri Lefebvre mobilises this term in his writing to indicate a radical orientation to society that offers an alternative to both efforts at the reform of capitalism and also the crude revolutionary statism of those inspired by Marxism – and in particular those whose Marxism has been grotesquely skewed by the authoritarian turn discernible in Leninism (Lefevbre, 2009).

By way of explanation,

> autogestion is not only a project of radically democratic governance but a conflictual, contradictory process through which participants continually engage in self-criticism, debate, deliberation, conflict, and struggle; it is not a fixed condition but a level of intense political engagement and "revolutionary spontaneity" that must "continually be enacted".
>
> (Brenner & Elden, 2009, p. 16)

This is referred to as self-management and workers control – and can be discerned in various events across history, from the foundation of cooperativism in Rochdale in 1844 through to the anti-Soviet uprisings in Hungary and Czechoslovakia in 1956 and 1968 respectively (Azzellini, 2022). Importantly, autogestion is not merely a replacement of extant means of control with another managerialist regime, such as you might see in contemporary capitalism with the embrace of practices such as 'Sociocracy' (Christian, 2016) and 'Holacracy' (van de Kamp, 2014), which serve to disguise and thereby preserve the current system. Instead, it can be said to be 'conceived as "self- gestation" – to create, control and provision with others one's own reality, hence to be collectively self-reliant and self- determining' (Vieta, 2016, p. 56).

The agency of change

Another contentious issue in respect to people's freedom and capacity for choice in the existential realm of the workplace is the way in which the idea of change has become reified and commodified. Existentialism sees change as arising out of the decisions and actions of people finding their way through the limited space and time into which they have been thrown. But companies are now increasingly populated by *soi-disant* change managers, champions, leaders, or agents, who are unchosen authority figures who seek to impose the unchallenged corporate vision on others at the behest of senior management.

This presupposes that change is something that has to be made to happen and actively forced on others, and not something intrinsic to human existence. To that extent, the use of the term 'change' in this context is something of a misnomer, with much more in common with a word such as 'compulsion'. The taken-for-granted practice of organisational change also assumes that it is possible to progress to an ideal state, and the achievement of pure essence of the notionally perfect company which exists apart from the lives of those having change imposed on them. In light of this, those who immerse themselves in the ideas and techniques of change management can be seen to be living their business lives in bad faith, denying themselves and those they engage with the experience of freedom and choice.

Some of these interpretations apply beyond just the nexus of corporate leadership and change management. We find ourselves thrown into workplace environments and compressed by the weight of them in light of wider social effects, such as the growth of massification. Two developments have proceeded along largely parallel paths: firstly, the growth and concentration of human society over time – particularly from the 19th century onwards – has seen us all become absorbed by the emergence of the mass, that shapeless agglomeration of people that is amenable to what Foucault called governmentality, a means of controlling people through engagement with populations. Secondly, this disappearing of the individual into the mass has taken place at a time when the political and juridical circumstances suggest that we have moved from being subjects to citizens (Lemke, 2019), and so are being framed as active agents in the lives of the body politic.

Clearly, absorption by the mass – whether willingly embraced or suffered as an implication of having to survive in the social – significantly impacts out respective capacity to assert ourselves existentially, in terms of making choice and expressing our freedom. An analysis flowing from this makes the following suggestion:

> The manual worker, the salaried employee, the doctor, the lawyer, do not as such combine to form the masses; each is a potential individual; but the proletariat, the general body of the medical profession, the teaching staff of a university – these respectively combine to form an

> articulated "mass" insofar as in actual fact the majority of the corporation decides the nature, the actions, the resolves of all its members.
> (Jaspers, 1931/2010, p. 41)

This provides the foundation for a tension, wherein the individual's desire for self-expression – our desire to actively 'be ourselves' – collides with our self-preservative needs. Exploring this conflictual context, Jaspers states that 'the urge to self-expression drives him into incalculable hazards which may render his means of livelihood perilously insecure' (Jaspers, 1931/2010, p. 45).

The workplace – despite much espoused corporate nonsense about the importance of our authentic selves presenting there and that the aim should be to bring one's whole self to work – is pre-eminent in preventing people from embracing their existence in good faith. And in the busyness of contemporary business, and the ceaseless drive for performance and productivity, it is apparent that '[t]he worker at the machine, concentrating upon immediate aims, has no time or inclination left for the contemplation of life as a whole' (Jaspers, 1931/2010, p. 52).

It's choice, Jim ... but not as we'd like to know it

To conclude this detailed exposition on the practicalities of living our lives in an authentic fashion when we're in the workplace, I wanted to reflect again on the insightful remarks made by one of the people who completed the survey. This person – marked as Paragraph J in the list earlier in the chapter – highlights the oft neglected fact that the relationship between the freedom to choose and the choices that we are then able to make is often in tension. In some instances, as they make clear, we are confronted by undesirable choices, which can leave us feeling trapped. It is also a reminder of the precept which I always thought was drawn from the work of Kierkegaard that there is no choice without sacrifice: as with Robert Frost's poem 'The Road Less Travelled' (Frost, 1916/1973), when faced with two paths splitting in the depths of a forest through which we are walking, it may ultimately not matter which one we choose, despite the fact that we might feel that it has made a massive difference. And, in opting for the one path, we are compelled to forego the other.

If we wish to live our lives in a way that is meaningful in respect to the existentialist notions of freedom and the capacity to have to make choices, we need to step into that position with an acknowledgement of the facticity that shapes our engagement with the world. We also need to feel content with the idea that we will reflexively engage with the challenge of existence and become aware of those instances where we are being authentic and those where perhaps we are living in bad faith. And there is a need for us all to actively deconstruct the corporate context in which we find ourselves, moving beyond the superficial understanding of the workplace to which we so often adhere and so recognise our agency – and the ways in which we are active agents in our workspace and its collective reality.

As John Higgins and I have expressly stated before, the key elements through which we can all find the ways in which to develop as human beings are threefold, namely criticality, reflexivity, and active exploration of our ethical self (Cole & Higgins, 2023, pp. 218–219). I had not realised until revisiting the philosophy for this book just how integral these three aspects of how best to live my life were to existentialism. And this also means that those who manage our organisations have a responsibility to live in the ways discussed herein themselves, while at the same time embracing the notion that they have a responsibility to make choices about the workplace that support people there to engage with their own freedom and to have space and time in which to make choices.

Simone de Beauvoir contests the very idea that a set of extant values can be seen to precede the judgment of the human agent as they seek to live their life in an existentialist way. She goes on to state that she and other existentialist writers 'think that it is possible for man to snatch the world from the darkness of absurdity, clothe it in significations, and project valid goals into it' (De Beauvoir, 1947/2020, p. 6). This applies as much to our place of work as it does to any other element of our lives. Definitionally, in choosing to live in an existentialist fashion, the following offers a useful definition of how we might experience it:

> The existentialist can be characterized through his capacity of facing anxiety, pursuing authenticity and recuperation of death. The attitude of the existentialist towards choice, decision and responsibility is exemplary. The existentialist knows the founding value of the choice, which has an open horizon and must be kept in pure potentiality. The decision that follows after choice, although narrowing the horizon of the existential subject, must be respected and brought in the field of continuity. Immersed in a culture of irresponsibility (in which the society, fate, God, the genes are always to blame), the existentialist will comprehend that the assignment of guilt, with all its seductive appearance, is ineffective, covering up the truth.
>
> (Bolea, 2014, p. 71)

Note

1 https://www.linkedin.com/posts/sophieedmond_i-hate-icebreaker-questions-with-a-passion-activity-7254123557138350083-Ngmz?utm_source=share&utm_medium=member_desktop([Accessed 23 October 24).

Bibliography

Admin. (2023, January 25). The Concept of Being-In-Itself and Being-For-Itself. Retrieved 20 November 2024, from *The Philosophy Room*: https://www.thephilroom.com/blog/2023/01/25/the-concept-of-being-in-itself-and-being-for-itself

Azzellini, D. (2022). Workers' control and self-management. In H. Veltmeyer, & P. Bowles (Eds.), *The Essential Guide to Critical Development Studies* (pp. 366–373). Abingdon: Routledge.

Birt, R. (1997). Existence, identity, and liberation. In L. R. Gordon (Ed.), *Existence in Black: An Anthology of Black Existential Philosophy* (pp. 205–213). New York: Routledge.

Block, P., & Koestenbaum, P. (2023). *Confronting Our freedom: Leading a Culture of Chosen Accountability and Belonging.* Hoboken, NJ: John Wiley & Sons.

Bolea, S. (2014). What is existentialism? A revision of contemporary definitions. *Studia UBB Philosophia, 59*(2), 63–72.

Brenner, N., & Elden, S. (2009). Introduction. State, space, world: Lefebvre and the survival of capitalism. In N. Brenner, & S. Elden (Eds.), *State, Space, World: Selected Essays – Henriu Lefevbre* (pp. 1–48). Minneapolis: University of Minnesota.

Bristol Leadership and Change Centre – UWE Bristol. (2021). *No Going Back! Learning and Unlearning about NHS Leadership Practice and Development in the Wake of COVID-19.* London & Bristol: NHS London Leadership Academy/UWE Bristol.

Christian, D. L. (2016). The seven steps of sociocracy – putting it all together. *Communities,* (Fall), 63–66.

Chung-Yan, G. A. (2010). The nonlinear effects of job complexity and autonomy on job satisfaction, turnover, and psychological well-being. *Journal of Occupational Health Psychology, 15*(3), 237–251.

Cole, M., & Higgins, J. (2022). *Leadership Unravelled: The Faulty Thinking Behind Modern Management.* Abingdon: Routledge.

Cole, M., & Higgins, J. (2023). *The Great Unheard at Work: Understanding Voice and Silence in Organisations.* Abingdon: Routledge.

Cox, G. (2011). *How to Be an Existentialist or How to get Real, Get a Grip and Stop Making Excuses*. London: Bloomsbury.
De Beauvoir, S. (1947/2018). *The Ethics of Ambiguity*. New York: Open Road Integrated Media.
De Beauvoir, S. (1947/2020). *What is Existentialism?* London: Penguin Books – Great Ideas.
Frost, R. (1916/1973). The Road Not Taken. In R. Frost, & I. Hamilton (Eds.), *Selected Poems* (p. 77). London: Penguin.
Fuller, R. W. (2004). *Somebodies and Nobodies: Overcoming the Abuse of Rank*. Gabriola Island, Canada: New Society Publishers.
Heidegger, M. (1993). Being and Time: Introduction. In D. Farrell Krell (Ed.), *Basic Writings from "Being and Time" (1927) to "The Task of Thinking" (1964)* (pp. 41–87). London: Routledge.
Henry, P. (1997). African and Afro-Caribbean existential philosophies. In L. R. Gordon (Ed.), *Existence in Black: An Anthology of Black Existential Philosophy* (pp. 13–36). New York: Routledge.
Hirschman, A. 0. (1970). *Exit, Voice, and Loyalty: Responses to Declines in Firms, Organizations, and States*. Cambridge, MA: Harvard University Press.
Jaspers, K. (1931/2010). *Man in the Modern Age*. Abingdon: Routledge.
Jones, C. (2003). Jacques Derrida. In S. Linstead (Ed.), *Organization Theory and Post-Modern Thought* (pp. 34–63). London: Sage.
Kierkegaard, S. (1843/1992). *Either/Or: A Fragment of Life*. London: Penguin.
Kierkegaard, S. (1980). *The Concept of Anxiety*. Princeton, NJ: Princeton University Press.
Killinger, J. (1961). Existentialism and human freedom. *The English Journal, 50*(5), 303–313.
Lawler, J. (2005). The essence of leadership? Existentialism and leadership. *Leadership, 1*(2), 215–231.
Lawler, J., & Ashman, I. (2012). Theorizing leadership authenticity: A Sartrean perspective. *Leadership, 8*(4), 327–344.
Lefevbre, H. (2009). Theoretical Problems of autogestion. In N. Brenner, & S. Elden (Eds.), *State, Space, World: Selected Essays – Henri Lefevbre* (pp. 138–152). Minneapolis: University of Minnesota Press.
Lemke, T. (2019). *Foucault's Analysis of Modern Governmentality: A Critique of Political Reason*. London: Verso.
Lyotard, J.-F. (1984). *The Postmodern Condition: A Report on Knowledge*. Manchester: Manchester University Press.
MacLaren, N. G., Yammarino, F. J., Dionne, S. D., Sayama, H., Mumford, M. D., Connelly, S.,... Ruark, G. A. (2020). Testing the babble hypothesis: Speaking time predicts leader emergence in small groups. *The Leadership Quarterly, 31*, 1–25.

Macquarrie, J. (1973). *Existentialism*. Harmondsworth: Penguin.

Maden, J. (2023, November). *Sartre's Waiter, 'Bad Faith', and the Harms of Inauthenticity*. Retrieved November 18, 2024, from https://philosophybreak.com/articles/sartre-waiter-bad-faith-and-the-harms-of-inauthenticity/

Mandalaywala, T. M., Amodio, D. M., & Rhodes, M. (2018). Essentialism promotes racial prejudice by increasing endorsement of social hierarchies. *Social Psychological and Personality Science, 9*(4), 461–469.

Marcel, G. (2018). *The Philosophy of Existence*. Providence, RI: Cluny Media.

Messenger, G. (2022,8 June). *Leadership for a Collaborative and Inclusive Future*. Retrieved 11 November 2024, from https://www.gov.uk/government/publications/health-and-social-care-review-leadership-for-a-collaborative-and-inclusive-future/leadership-for-a-collaborative-and-inclusive-future

Quinn, P. L. (2010). Sin and Original Sin. In C. Taliaferro, P. Draper, & P. L. Quinn (Eds.), *A Companion to Philosophy of Religion* (pp. 614–621). Chichester: Wiley-Blackwell.

Rea, M. C. (2007). The metaphysics of Original Sin. In P. Van Inwagen, & D. Zimmerman (Eds.), *Persons – Human and Divine* (pp. 319–356). Oxford: Clarendon Press/Oxford Uiversity Press.

Reason, J. (2008). *The Human Contribution: Unsafe Acts, Accidents and Heroic Recoveries*. Farnham: Ashgate.

Roberts, J. (2011). *The Necessity of Errors*. London: Verso.

Saragih, S. (2011). The effects of job autonomy on work outcomes: Self efficacy as an intervening variable. *International Research Journal of Business Studies, 4*(3), 203–215.

Sartre, J.-P. (1943/1957). *Being and Nothingness: An Essay on Phenomenological Ontology*. London: Methuen & Co Ltd.

Sartre, J.-P. (1965/1993). *Essays in Existentialism*. (W. Baskin, Ed.) New York: Citadel Press & Kensington Publishing Corp.

Theory of Enchantment. (2024). *Theory of Enchantment – About (The Essence of Our Work)*. Retrieved 4 December 2024, from https://www.theoryofenchantment.com/about

Ungar-Sargon, B. (2020, 20 July). *A New Intelligentsia is Pushing Back Against Wokeness*. Retrieved December 3, 2024, from Forward: https://forward.com/opinion/451099/a-new-intelligentsia-is-pushing-back-against-wokeness

van de Kamp, P. (2014). Holacracy: A radical approach to organizational design. In H. Dekkers, W. Leeuwis, & I. Plantevin (Eds.), *Elements of the Software Development Process: Influences on Project Success and Failure* (pp. 13–25). Amsterdam: University of Amsterdam.

Vereen, L. G., Lemberger-Truelove, T., Hannon, M. D., Howard, N., & Burt, I. (2017). Black existentialism: Extending the discourse on meaning and existence. *Journal of Humanistic Counseling, 56*(April), 72–84.

Verkuyten, M. (2003). Discourses about ethnic group (de-)essentialism: Oppressive and progressive aspects. *British Journal of Social Psychology, 42*(3), 371–391.
Vieta, M. (2016). Autogestion: Prefiguring a 'new cooperativism' and the 'labour commons'. In C. DuRand (Ed.), *Moving Beyond Capitalism* (pp. 55–63). London: Routledge.
Wahl, J. (1959/2019). *Philosophies of Existence: An introduction to the Basic Thought of Kierkegaard, Heidegger, Jaspers, Marcel, Sartre*. Abingdon: Routledge.
Witzel, M. (2022). The Power of Humble: Re-imagining the Power of Leaders after COVID-19. In M. Witzel (Ed.), *Post-Pandemic Leadership: Exploring Solutions to a Crisis* (pp. 127–135). Abingdon: Routledge.

Time at work 3

We are all meat clocks

At the end of March 2020, I had my 60th birthday. When I turned 40 and 50 friends had persuaded me to celebrate with a party. So, for those two events, I hired the downstairs space of a little bar called Café Koha, which sits behind one of the entrances to Leicester Square underground station in London. I enjoyed both events and felt positive about having brought people together for my birthday party. But, as I approached 60, I found it especially difficult to be positive. It felt like I was crossing a threshold into an altogether different space, where time wasn't just passing but could be felt to be running out.

In the end, I began to plan for a party. In late 2019, I booked a large room in a local hotel and began to send out the 'save the date' emails and then formal invitations. It looked as though around 60 people were planning to come and I started to bracket off the idea of turning 60 and focused instead on the fun to be had with friends at a big social event, with drink, food, and music.

As the date approached, the media was full of discussion about the coronavirus that had emerged in China and was now enveloping the world. I recall chatting to a friend at work who had just returned from a holiday in Italy, where the virus was rife and putting unbearable pressure on its health care systems. I told him to go home and work from there, until he was reassured that he had not caught Covid-19 on his travels. Not long after that, we were all told to start working from home.

My wife and I agonised about the party. In the end, we pulled the plug … and not long after the country was tightly locked down in an effort

DOI: 10.4324/9781003592624-3

to minimise transmission and avoid putting intolerable pressure on the health-care system and the people who worked in it. We can too easily forget the drumbeat reports of ever increasing numbers of hospitalisations and the sense of a failing system, with oxygen in short supply in our acute hospitals. I felt as though the veneer of civilisation was falling away – and we would be confronting an appalling social collapse. I grew certain that we were facing an unspeakable disaster.

In those early months of the pandemic, death was suddenly front and centre of both public discourse and private conversation. We were advised daily of the numbers who had died or were in hospital in intensive care, being ventilated. For most of our lives, we silently recognise the presence of death and yet find ways to push it aside to prevent it from dominating our thoughts so that we might focus positively on living. Now we were no longer able to ignore that 'in the midst of life we are in death' (Church of England, 2024). Meanwhile public health messages stopped us from thinking of ourselves as human beings and cast us instead as vectors, means by which the virus might spread. We were constantly told that by our actions we might kill others and that others would be able to kill us. We were merely conduits through which this pernicious curl of RNA in a protein envelope could infect and affect us quite drastically.

The convergence of these two events – reaching 60 and the appearance of a dangerous illness – prompted a high degree of existential angst in me, something I am still working with a psychotherapist to address. Moreover, the opportunity thereafter to step out of the consuming busyness of a salaried life amplified the space for such angst. Suddenly, I found that I had time on my hands … and I was brought up short by the visceral recognition of how much of my life to date had been spent at work.

Existentialism focuses heavily on the notion of temporality. We are thrown into the world – and the one certainty as we land is that our time is limited, a fact we try to ignore even though its denial may well be an act of bad faith. Death has been referred to in terms of existential psychology as an 'absent presence', meaning that we hold within us both an acknowledgement of the past and a recognition of a future, which ends with our passing. We live our lives, knowingly or otherwise, between the past that we have fashioned for ourselves through freedom and choice and a finite future (Feifel, 1969, p. 59). In practical terms, this can be taken to mean that:

> A man's birth is an uncontrollable event in his life, but the manner of his departure from life bears a definite relation to his philosophy of life and death. We are mistaken in considering a purely biologic event.

> Life is not comprehended truly or lived fully unless the idea of death is grappled with honestly.
>
> (Feifel, 1969, p. 70)

Tick tock ... slow down clock!

I often wonder how many people are content in their working lives. My career comes in two phases: an initial 33 years spent doing work to the best of my ability but deriving no joy or motivation from it ... and the final eight years where I discovered that it was possible to derive pleasure from the work that socio-economic necessity required me to do.

This mirrors my experience of formal education. I saw no point to what was going on during my primary and secondary education and felt no inspiration to do well. Nothing that teachers confronted me with made me feel the least bit engaged. However, eight years after escaping the clutches of a deadening curriculum and a horde of bullies, I found myself actively working to get back into formal education, this time to study industrial relations and trade union studies, a topic that truly, madly, deeply interested me.

One of the things Covid threw in my face was something I'd actively ignored during those first 33 years of work, namely, "Why do I spend so much of my life toiling away in jobs that I cannot get excited about, for organisations and people for whom I have limited (if any) respect, when life itself is relatively short?" The presence of death in the form of the virus pushed that question to the forefront of my thinking, even though by then I was doing work that I deeply enjoyed. I was haunted by the existentialist query as to why I had spent so much of my time pursuing things that simply did not make me happy.

This is an instance of facticity: we are thrown into a prevailing socio-economic and cultural circumstance which we are compelled to experience. We are born into the 'way things are', which in turn limits our capacity to imagine ways in which things might be other than they are. Moreover, we know that where people have envisaged and pursued alternative systems, they have often turned out to be even less appealing than the status quo they were seeking to replace. The daily grind in a capitalist system is preferable to the gulag, working for a wage is better than the surveillant attentions and punishments of a police state.

In fact, the existentialist question takes us beyond the idea of how we live now and with what we might replace it. It observes that we each find ourselves for a brief moment spinning on a pale blue dot in the middle of an unimaginably large universe, beyond which we are compelled to imagine nothingness. Without the comfort of religious faith, we may feel compelled to confront these circumstances as being absurd, as Albert Camus did. His was a distinctive take on the world which can be seen to be more despairing than that of his contemporaries Sartre and De Beauvoir, who rejected the nihilistic notion of the innate absurdity of life. Instead, they argued that individuals can actively find meaning and purpose in their time in the world.

In reviewing these different positions, the following analysis is offered: 'Like Sartre in *Nausea*, [Camus] points out that mostly we don't see the fundamental problem of life because we don't stop to think about it. We get up, commute, work, eat, work, commute, sleep' (Bakewell, 2016, p. 149). Occasionally, the reality of how we live breaks through, which for Camus leads us to question why we persist when faced with the absurdity of life. To an extent, his perspective in this regard is pithily expressed by the character Josey in the Tony Hancock film from 1961 called *The Rebel*. In it, the Tony Hancock character abandons his work as a clerk to pursue a career as an artist, which takes him to Paris where he is immersed in a milieu that patently references existentialism and where Josey opines, 'We only live in the present; there is no future. Why kill time when you can kill yourself?' (Day, 1961).

It is worth bearing in mind that Camus codified his thoughts at the close of the Second World War, in the shadow of the blanket bombing of civilian populations in cities like Coventry and Dresden, and the industrialised and bureaucratic systems that had processed the deaths of millions. This suggests that 'In the face of such far-reaching misery, the concepts of absolute values had dissipated like those hellish clouds of smoke emerging from the chimneys of Treblinka' (Cavanaugh, 2024, p. 113). Camus in the face of this and the emergence of nuclear weaponry, alongside the certainty of death, concluded that existence was absurd.

This became a philosophy of despair, where he compared human life to the experience of Sisyphus, the mythical fallen king compelled to push a rock up a hill each day, only for it to roll down to the bottom again each night. In making this comparison, Camus seems to suggest that:

> The burdens of life in this world are one's boulder, and all the struggles one encounters have no apparent meaning or purpose since they will be repeated tomorrow. Life is little more than a series of choices, defining moments that dictate how one's days would progress, without being able to alter the human condition.
>
> (Cavanaugh, 2024, p. 113)

If we concede that freedom and choice are significant aspects of being a human – and to eschew that responsibility is to live inauthentically – then the absurdity of life should be a fleeting thought, subsumed by the agency we have to weave meaning and purpose into our existence. In contrast to Camus, at least one existentialist writer – with first-hand experience of the horror of the Nazi concentration camps – argues that 'Ultimately, man should not ask what the meaning of his life is, but rather he must recognise that it is *he* who is asked' (Frankl, 1946/2004, p. 113) Emphasis in original].

Instead of wondering about the meaning of life, we are being urged here to actively create meaning through the living of our lives. Which means, according to Frankl, that this meaning is different for each of us ... and may be different from moment to moment. Hence, we need to surrender the search for the meaning of life: instead, we should work to create meaning from the life that we choose to lead.

Clock watching at work

The challenge here is that so much of our time is consumed by the world of work. Increasingly, that commitment extends beyond the 9 to 5, and across what was once considered the weekend but now ends up merely as a *weekextension*. It is Marx who drove us to the conclusion that humankind lives to work, although this feels to be more of a political than an ontological observation, especially when it is argued as follows:

> Marx holds that work has the potential to be something creative and fulfilling. He consequently rejects the view of work as a necessary evil, denying that the negative character of work is part of our fate, a universal fact about the human condition that no amount of social change could remedy. Indeed, productive activity, on Marx's account, is a central element in what it is to be a human being, and self-realisation through work is a vital component of human flourishing. That he thinks that work—in a different form of society—could be creative and fulfilling, perhaps explains the intensity and scale of Marx's condemnation of contemporary economic arrangements and their transformation of workers into deformed and "dehumanised" beings.
>
> (Wolff & Leopold, 2021)

Without the compulsion of the economic each of us would need to find for ourselves a way of spending the limited time we have that was satisfying and personally meaningful, but this might not necessarily be thought of as work. Instead, we find ourselves trapped in our working lives, dancing to a tune we played no part in composing, where the experience of personal choice about how we spend our time is taken away from us.

In some instances, of course, immersing oneself in the presumption and practicalities of paid employment is a way of distracting ourselves from Camus' absurdity of existence (Camus, 1955/1991). This distraction can in turn be seen as an act of bad faith, a means of not having to confront the nature of our existence. When one takes the Sisyphean myth as a reflection of the absurdity of both human existence and the futility of paid employment in a capitalist society into which we've all been thrown, we are confronted by the inescapability of absurdity.

This leaves us with a profound and deeply disruptive question, namely: in recognition of the finite time of my existence, am I using it in a way that is both personally honest and potentially rewarding? This is a scary question, because – if I answer it honestly – it may mean that I have squandered much of my time in pursuit of activity that is not of my choosing. Of course, most of us make a deal with the capitalist devil, by taking an instrumentalist view of the world of work, promoting the precept that 'I work to live, I do not live to work.'

When I left school and started work in 1976 I puttered along as a shop assistant, a window dresser, and an operating theatre orderly for around eight years, before heading back to full time education for a further nine years. I had fun with the people I worked with in all of those jobs but cannot suggest that what I was paid for offered me any great sense of meaning or purpose.

It was during my time as a theatre porter when I experienced an important shift in my sense of self. I became an auto-didact like Sartre's character Roquentin (Sartre, 2020), and discovered things in the world that – unlike every school subject – genuinely intrigued and interested me. But the workplace was merely a setting for that self-inquiry as opposed to something that actually prompted it. And the benefits that derived from that came at considerable cost, in terms of seeing me locked into work for over 40 hours a week, clocking in every day at 8am, using old fashioned cards and a timeclock in a corridor behind the hospital kitchens. If you arrived three or more minutes late on any day, you were quartered, meaning that they immediately docked a quarter of an hour's pay from your wages that week. I quickly came to the conclusion that I could cope with losing 15 minutes' worth of money … and that, if I was going to be quartered, it made more sense to roll into work at around 8.14am. Eventually, the administration cottoned on to the way in which I was exercising some resistance to their regime and I was embroiled in the first of quite a few disciplinaries.

Even when, years later, I discovered motivation and engagement at a deeply personal level from the work I was paid to do, I was haunted by the spectre in the shadows, whispering, "Why are you eating away at this precious resource of your limited time in the world doing work that someone else expects you to do in exchange for a bank account full of cash?" It seems I am not alone in this regard, particularly in the light of recent history.

Back to the present

It is reported that there is an increasing trend for young people to reject paid employment and to embrace the status of being a Neet, an acronym for 'not in education, employment, or training'. Alongside this there seems to be a growing number of slightly older people joining this Neet sub-culture, both in the UK and across Europe. The article that shares these insights quotes the following story of one such individual:

> After starting out as a car salesman ten years ago, Morgan, now 30, was forced out of work by depression and an illness that took him in and out of hospital. When he recovered, the pandemic had shut his industry down: he opted out of work, using the time to teach himself how to repair old cars and post videos online. "My time to develop my interests was worth more than I could make working, even if it wasn't making me money", he says. But eventually the bills began to pile up. "I was put out on the street for unpaid rent. I lived in my car for a few days before a friend took me in. I'm lucky that's where I am today."
>
> (Zand, 2024)

This foregrounds for me the impact of recent events on the certainties and beliefs to which humanity has cleaved for centuries. As Simon Western argues, 'The Covid pandemic is a warning; it is an amplifier of what already exists. It warns us to lose our attachment and devotion to human omnipotence, and to traverse the fantasy that the ethos of modernity can save us' (Western, 2023, p. 144). This requires us to abandon the central myth about which John Higgins and I speak in respect to our analysis of the social context of contemporary leadership, namely that 'all is fixable' (Cole & Higgins, 2022), and simultaneously – according to Western – 'to learn to live with precarity, fragility, connectedness, and interdependence in new ways' (Western, 2023, p. 144).

Workplace shifts that shake its foundations

The reference to 'precarity' is a reminder of Judith Butler's distinction between *precariousness* – a shared state of all human beings in light of our interlinked presence in the world – and *precarity* – a particular experience of unprotectedness and uncertainty experience by marginalised groups (Butler, 2009). A research report undertaken by academics at University College London published in 2024 found that

> ... between 2009 and 2022 some 10–11.7% of the workforce could be classified as precarious workers i.e. workers in a state of *precarity*. Contrary to expectations, our assessment found the proportion of precarious workers to be remarkably stable over the studied time period. Precarious workers are more likely to be female, younger and working class, to work in hospitality, retail or construction, and are half as likely to work in unionised workplaces
>
> (Pósch, et al., 2024)

A rich picture of the negativity that accompanies this precarity, in terms of how people who find themselves in these circumstances experience the situation, is partially revealed in the following statement from a detailed research report on the topic for the Trade Unions Congress:

> As compared to permanent employees, workers in casual employment are more likely: to be young, non-white and employed in an elementary occupation; experience lower job satisfaction and life satisfaction; have perceived low employment security; and higher levels of anxiety and depression and are more likely to anticipate losing their jobs and withdraw from the labour market.
>
> (Newsome et al., 2018, p. 7)

This report also noted how employment of this sort – while sometimes presented as offering a flexibility liked by those who prefer a less formalised relationship with the world of work – is also associated with a wide range of negative outcomes, especially in terms of the balance of power between management and employees. This played out in 'draconian performance management regimes' (Newsome et al., 2018, p. 8), which seemingly provided a pretext for actual bullying and harassment of workers by managers. The fear of precarity also then rippled out, impacting the wider workforce, not just those in precarious employment. Those with full-time formal contracts sensed the consequences of drifting into a more informal economy if they did anything that put at risk the secure job they were currently in.

This suggests that for many people in our economy working life continues to be less secure and satisfying than it is promoted as being, with economic orthodoxy forcing people into decidedly fragile and unstable circumstances. To make sense of this and the emergence of so-called *indie unions*, such as the Independent Workers' Union of Great Britain (IWGB, 2025), it is argued that:

> Structural transformations such as outsourcing, fragmentation, decentralization, tertiarization and financialization have resulted in job degradation and increased precarity for a growing number of workers – especially if migrant. For low paid precarious migrant workers this situation has been made even worse by the development of a hostile immigration environment. The labour movement has struggled to navigate these transformations, and large unions have lost their ability to retain members and protect their deteriorating conditions.
>
> (Però, 2020)

Resonant with the challenge of precarity, a survey commissioned by the insurance company Admiral suggests that of a sample of 2000 18–27-year-olds, 75 per cent were committed to seeking long-term employment as opposed to the portfolio career previously seen as a key requirement of the Gen Z categorisation (Beal, 2025). Here we see another essentialist distortion of people's lived experience, an approach that denies the way in which as individuals we make our way through our lives in favour of the idea that a key marker can be used to define who we are (or should be). It seems self-evident that using our date of birth to define how we see, understand, and participate in the world is about as rigorous as an astrological horoscope – and serves as an act of depersonalisation (Ronan, 2022).

If we consider life at work, there are clearly challenges in respect to precarity which affect a relatively small number of people in terms of the overall workforce in a country such as the UK. But there is a more widespread challenge that arises from the nature of contemporary capitalism in regard to the purpose, nature, and quality of the work we find ourselves actually doing. This arises from the insights of the late David Graeber, who uses the term *bullshit jobs*, by which he means:

> [A] bullshit job is a form of paid employment that is so completely pointless, unnecessary, or pernicious that even the employee cannot justify its existence, even though, as part of the conditions of employment, the employee feels obliged to pretend that this is not the case.
>
> (Graeber, 2019, pp. 9–10)

His research, as a professor of anthropology, led him to suggest five types of work that fell under this category in contemporary society: *flunky jobs*, which aimed to make someone else look important; *what goons do*, a category that highlights occupations that only persist because everyone else does them; *the duct tapers*, roles that only exist because of a structural or systemic error in organisations that needs to be under constant repair; *the box tickers*, who collate data that allows organisations to pretend that they're doing things that they're not actually doing; and lastly there are *taskmasters*, of which there is one group who dish out work to others and another that keeps bullshit in organisational circulation (Graeber, 2019, pp. 28–58)

Reading Graeber left me somewhat disconsolately thinking that the activity that filled my working life was a prime example of duct taping, a conclusion I'd reached when I wrote a book critiquing Organisation Development as a field of practice and my role in it – and which posited a different way in which I intended to try to work from that point on (Cole, 2020).

Graeber's analysis has a political orientation, whereas I am concerned with how each of us in (or around) corporate entities experiences our immersion in such a working life. To be locked into a job that does not appear to have a purpose other than to keep us preoccupied would seem to deny us the opportunity to live in good faith. There have been times in my career when I have found myself gloomily reflecting that whether I turned up in my job the next day or not would not register with the world, a reflection that was amplified as I moved further away from doing the job and into managing people who did the job.

This is why, in my organisational practice, I so often focus on *leadership distance* (Cole & Higgins, 2023, pp. 221–222), the idea that a gulf quickly opens up between the business of the business and the position of the senior managers at the pinnacle of the company. This represents not just a practical challenge in terms of organisational connectiveness and communication but an existential one as well, wherein the further we move away from what needs to actually happen to create goods or service that are needed by a client base, the more we end up feeling disconnected from meaning. This gap of leadership distance both inhibits organisational effectiveness and makes it more difficult for us as individuals to feel fulfilled by how we are spending our time.

Our temporality and the way in which so much of our lives is spent at work make the issue of what we find ourselves doing in these circumstances all the more important. The idea that there is something natural about the way in which our society and its underlying economy is organised is being increasingly contested by trends explored above, with some people turning away from work while others are seeking out a more solid foundation in respect to their employment and where that takes place. And if we start to query the very nature of the work that we are asked to do, then the picture becomes even more complicated.

Told what to do, how to do it … and now where it needs to happen

There is the ongoing post-pandemic discussion about where it is best for people to work. Covid-19 encouraged us into interestingly changed circumstances in respect to how we could get our work done. The effect seems to have been so profound as to leave many people wondering why they had worked in the way in which they had worked for so long. It feels as though we all began by asking how and where we could complete the tasks expected of us in the light of lockdown … and, in some instances, to quietly and privately question the very nature of what it was that we were being asked to do.

Despite my submersion in intense anxiety in the face of the pandemic, I was able to recognise the exquisite shift that occurred with the arrival of the coronavirus not just in my working life but life in general. Before Covid, I schlepped joylessly into Central London five days a week on packed and unreliable commuter trains. I would leave the house early and arrive home late, an absentee father for my young son during the working week.

I think for many that shift in work-life balance opened an unexpected opportunity to interrogate what it meant to work for money. I am aware, of course, that for some people, that change from a location-based working life to one that pivoted around the home was problematic. Some who lived alone found homeworking isolating … and those who lived in busy properties struggled to find a comfortable space in which to work. Even I found myself carefully navigating the intrusion of work into my domestic setting.

At the end of the 2024, Christmas holidays, a friend and I talked about the upcoming return to work. He admitted he was 'Not massively looking forward to the office tomorrow'. After his first day back I asked him how it had been and told him that I had been writing this chapter about how much of our time we squander on paid employment. He responded, 'It wasn't too bad in the end. Squandering time on paid employment is one thing. Squandering time (and money) on commuting to paid employment is quite another.'

The pandemic offered us an opportunity for a little more personal control in our lives and a means to wriggle free of the surveillant nature of the contemporary workplace. However, for every action there is an equal and opposite reaction – and the assertion ascribed to the South American revolutionary Regis Debray underscores that by observing that *the revolution revolutionises the counter-revolution*. Technology was an economic saviour as we all faced lockdown, insofar as Zoom and Teams allowed us to continue to connect and work together. But managers, disconcerted that they were unable to justify themselves to themselves and to those around them by sitting on the shoulders of those who reported to them, quickly capitalised on a shadow side to technology.

This shadow showed itself through its capacity to support the surveillance of those working in their own homes and at a distance from the factory floor or office suite (Vitak & Zimmer, 2023), which in turn led some researchers to express concerns about the development of algorithmic management (Mateescu & Nguyen, 2019) and the emergence of what they called a Covid pandemic panopticon (Aloisi & De Stefano, 2022). A structure of surveillance which further restricted people's capacity to exercise choice, and create personal meaning, within the facticity of work.

Fading opportunity

The space for work to be a useful distraction is getting squeezed, especially for the managerial classes. Organisations are embracing the idea of flattening their bureaucracies and ripping out the need for managerial posts. The potential to bide one's time in the absurdity of one's current role in order to seize in time a subsequent opportunity to move up the hierarchy through promotion to a more senior – oftentimes managerial – appointment is fast disappearing.

This has led some commentators to wonder whether management as a career might be disappearing. In the crude individualism of the neo-liberal world view, self-management and self-leadership are being promoted as the way in which management can be set aside organisationally. Clearly, however, these companies can make managers disappear … but managerialism persists, asserting itself through the active promotion of the illusion of workplace autonomy at the individual level and the oppressive supervisory presence of the corporate notion of the workplace team. One finds teams in sports settings … but the importation of the term into the business context sees it applied to groups of workers to elicit their compliance to the corporate norms without having to have a manager breathing down their necks. There are very few people who would want to be openly described as not being a good team player, so it is an ideal means by which to ensure that employees internalise the corporate expectations and culture of the companies in which they find themselves (Cole, 2020, pp. 96–110).

There's obviously a bottom-line payoff to a company from stripping out layers of middle management, demanding instead that people take responsibility for actively managing themselves and subtly overseeing one another, and presenting that as a positive and humanising development of autonomy, something which people are said to crave in the workplace. Offering a concessionary amount of limited liberty in this way creates an illusion of meaningful control across the workforce, heading off possible demands for greater freedom and the sort of workers' control that – as we saw earlier – Henri Lefebvre termed autogestion (Lefebvre, 1966), which is said to be spontaneous and localised collective action that is 'a means of struggle, which clears the way; and … a means for the reorganization of society, which transforms it from bottom to top, from everyday life to the State' (Lefebvre, 1966, p. 149). And this promotion of a sanitised version of autonomy might also be argued to further veil the absurdity of work in a capitalist workplace.

The challenging picture for those investing their trust in a system of work that in principle is seeking to be fair, engaging, and inclusive is summarised very neatly in the following:

> In 2025, it's predicted that 1 in 10 management roles will be filled by Gen Z. But that's a complicated statistic, when management jobs are going the way of the milk man and the fax machine. *Forbes* highlights the stark reality of white-collar job cuts, with middle-management positions being systematically eliminated at organizations like Google, Meta, UPS and others. Indeed, middle management positions accounted for nearly a third of layoffs in 2023 … That's bad news for Gen Z workers seeking guidance, mentoring and oversight. Or a white-collar job in management. Is management a disappearing career?
>
> (Westfall, 2025)

Meanwhile, *Forbes* was reporting a few months earlier that Gen Z could be seen to be turning its back on traditional management, eschewing basic authority – such as that which might be seen to derive from positional power – in favour of expertise. A figure of 52 per cent of people in this group were said in the article to be actively avoiding management because, according to Lucy Bisset, a director at the company that commissioned the survey, it is a corporate pursuit that is too strongly associated with 'stress, limited autonomy, and poor work-life balance'. It is also said to be a sign of a rejection of traditional hierarchy (Pontefract, 2024).

The broad sweep of time in organisations

Let's head back here to a more philosophical consideration of how we balance our existence with the pressures and expectations of our working life. Our awareness of our temporality means that our personal thoughts about time and its passage are critical to our existence. We also find ourselves enmeshed in thinking about time that is not necessarily our own, but which deeply affects how we are in the world and how we think about it.

I will start by observing that the corporate notion of temporality is grotesquely distorted. It is a perspective on time, its passage, and its phasing, that seems distanced from our experience of being. For most of human history, time was experienced in broad brush strokes: the overall pace of our lives was dictated by the seasons, while – at a more detailed level – it would have been defined by dawn, noon, and dusk. Our understanding of these markers of the day would have been dictated by our experience of where we saw the sun: rising in the east, finding its highest point, and then slipping away in the west.

The appearance of machines, such as spinning jennies and steam engines, marked the start of industrialisation. Those technologies facilitated the emergence of large towns and cities full of factories, where people were thrown together. The productive process was broken down into a plethora of sub-tasks … and those working in the factories were allocated responsibility for undertaking just one or two elements of that overall procedure, eliminating the holistic view of creative activity that they might previously have enjoyed.

This mechanisation of human activity was premised on the application of one crucial and relatively small machine, namely the clock. Timepieces had existed for some time, but the massification of productive endeavour was founded on the emergence of the clock (Martineau, 2016). This technology segmented the day into the minutest units, all the better to control the new industrial workforce. The appearance of scientific management as the critical means of taking possession of the lives of those thrown together in the factories was built on the practice of the localised investigation, of the interrelationship of time and motion. And we remain caught in this clock bound way of being in respect to the ongoing discussions that dominate economic debate about the linked challenges of growth and productivity.

Latterly, we find the mechanisation of time acknowledging our finitude and placing it in front of us. There was a time, not so long ago, when people used technological applications such as a Death Clock to calculate when their passing was likely to occur. This seemed to take understanding temporality to a whole new level, where these people tried to create some certainty in regard to their demise, albeit an entirely artificial forecast of something that is actually unknowable. Alongside this, the global population – particularly during the Cold War and its threat of nuclear destruction – has found itself confronted by the Doomsday Clock, an assessment by a group of scientists of how close the Earth is to an existential catastrophe, which can be found on the internet at: https://thebulletin.org/doomsday-clock. As I wrote this section, I checked where we find ourselves on the basis of this calculation – and was disconcerted to discover the clock on 28 January 2025 was set at 89 seconds to midnight.

This development marks a shift from an understanding of human existence as something embedded in the ebb and flow of the ecosystem of which human beings are clearly part to an instrumentalisation of time as a means of maximising the extraction of value out of people's endeavours in return for a pay packet … and laying down the key column of managerialism, namely exercising power over this most fundamental aspect of being alive and thereby dictating how people are allowed to live out the literal time of their lives.

The contemporary economy has replaced the seasons as a key means of mapping the passing of time with a focus on three phases. First, in corporate settings, the notion of the *past* is seen as a graveyard of myriad mistakes or – in a few instances – as a halcyon period that has somehow become lost. It is always presented as being behind us, thereby denying the potential for careful and meaningful reflection on what took place and the linked development of informed options as to how things might be approached in the moment.

This archiving of the past and the associated refusal to engage with it came up in a recent discussion around the theme of spaciousness in the world – and in particular in the organisations in which we work (Reitz & Higgins, 2025). In drawing attention to the dominance of 'doing' (and being seen to be doing) in life in general and in business in particular, the authors make the case for embracing a spacious mode, which they take to be 'characterised by an expansive, exploratory attention where dynamic interdependencies and relationships are foregrounded and where, in the absence of pressure from immediate expectations, a different quality of insight becomes possible' (Reitz & Higgins, 2025, p. 5).

For me, this work explores how refusing people at work the opportunity for spaciousness squeezes out doubt in human presence and practice, which is crucial in terms of making sense of the world and so enabling meaningful choice. It makes living in good faith impossible. Indeed, I would argue that doubt and resistance are two unacceptable states in organisational life … and that giving oneself permission to pause, in terms of granting space and time in which to think about life, reflect on it in detail, and come to tentative conclusions is, in fact, an important act of resistance to the dominant discourse and ways of being.

Alongside the past, the second focus of economic time is on the *future*, which is proposed as a glowing picture of goodness. Corporate settings cleave to the notion of the 'vision' as a vital guiding star for the company. It is argued that these images of how the senior leadership expect to see future time unfold are central to providing direction to the firm and those who work in it. In that regard, the conceit of designing a future to then be strategically pursued is both hubristic, insofar as it suggests that what is about to unfold is both predictable and controllable, and oppressive, in that it relegates the agency and existence of all of those who pledge themselves to be part of that workforce to the silence of the shadows.

This image of the future is created by senior managers who drift free from the practicalities of the workplace and describe it in terms of the epiphenomenal pursuits of crafting visions, missions, values, and strategies. These people sit atop, and apart from, those working to sustain its infrastructure, which get things done that need to be done for the firm to be successful. Importantly, in terms of thinking existentially, it reminds us that positional power in companies ends up defining time for everyone else around them – and, in so doing, imposes meaning on them. This dominant focus on what is just around the corner silences the voices of others, who also have experience to draw on and could find meaning in work if they were able to contribute to an understanding of the future.

The third phase of time in organisational life feels to be the most important, yet it tends to be overshadowed by the rejected past and the dominant narrative of the future. This is the *present*, the moment in which we actually find ourselves living our lives, from the instant that we find ourselves thrown into existence to the point at which we die. Companies often pivot back and forth, from past to future and back again, over and over … but rarely acknowledge that their workforce are living their lives in the present moment.

At this point it is worth considering an existentialist meme that can be found in a wide range of social media settings. A person is sitting on a park bench, underneath a tree, speaking with an oversized owl. The sun is setting for the day behind them, having dropped halfway down past the horizon and it casts an orange glow across the sky and clouds. The person asks the owl, 'Why is happiness so elusive?' The owl replies, 'Because you look for it in the future instead of the present.' If we allow our working lives to be torn between the past and the future, we are failing to acknowledge that we live our lives in the present … and that is where our focus (and that of those for whom we work) needs to be.

Taking time to task

At the personal level we can be said to be left with three questions as to how best to navigate our existence in the specific context of the workplace.

First, we must consider *Our Personal Time*: this opens with the inquiry 'How do I wish to spend my life? What can I do to find my way to where I want to be?' Facticity renders this complicated, for we are forced to face the common sensical qualities of the extant regime of socio-economic expectations – and, if we opt to abandon it, we must acknowledge that it is failing to offer that we truly need to live the life we've been thrown into. Considering this as a factor in how we choose to be in the world – and keeping that consideration under constant review – represents a positive step away from the allure of bad faith. It also creates space where not only do we consider whether we choose either to embrace or to eschew the rat race but we also consider in detail how we want to run that marathon on a moment-by-moment basis.

We may find ourselves immersed in what one writer describes as a Deferred Life Plan, where we put up with things that bring us no joy on the assumption that we will find happiness later (Komisar, 2001). Drawing on a rich history of living at a senior level in American corporate life, Komisar argues that:

> The Deferred Life Plan … dictates that we divorce who we are and what we care about from what we do in that first step. By distancing the real person from her actions, all manner of bad behaviour is justified in the name of business … Fueled by ambition, we hope that in the end we will be judged by our accomplishments, not by who we are.
>
> (Komisar, 2001, p. 83)

This seems a clear indication of people living in bad faith, creating a work environment that is potentially deeply uncomfortable for everyone who is part of that context, including themselves. This existentialist quality to the experience of steering a course in the constraining circumstances of paid employment can be put thus: 'And then there is the most dangerous risk of all – the risk of spending your life not doing what you want on the bet you can buy yourself the freedom to do it later' (Komisar, 2001, p. 154).

Second, we must wonder about *Activist Time*. Specifically, we must ask ourselves if the way that humanity currently lives feels untenable and unsustainable, how can we move beyond critique to a new way of thinking about what it is to exist? It's not about supplanting one model for another, it's about a dialogue about how humans could live better in light of their central, time bound, existential limitation. Are we happy to accept the way things are, rather than embrace an authentic way of living? Or are we willing to think through how existence could be freed from the restrictions placed upon it by the extant socio-economic system? Not the easy option ... but potentially the most profound and authentic one.

Two recent developments are ways to critique our present situation, with the potential to liberate us from our absorption in an unthinking commitment to working as work has always been done.

Neither of these involve mere tweaking of the ways of the economic world. The first of these genuinely radical ideas is the introduction of a Universal Basic Income, which – according to the work-oriented think tank Autonomy – can be understood as:

> [A] proposal to provide all citizens with a regular guaranteed payment, which may vary from modest to generous. Another way of putting it is that basic income establishes a guaranteed income floor. With a basic income in place, no citizen will have to worry about dropping beneath this floor. An important feature of basic income is that it is unconditional, meaning it has no strings attached. The payment is the same for everyone, regardless of their employment, family or financial situation, and citizens are not forced to do anything in return for payments... Basic income can help people have more autonomy over their work choices, improve health by increasing income security, and insulate citizens in times of economic turmoil – be it the Covid pandemic, or future economic disruptions caused by forces like climate change and AI.
>
> (Frayne & Goodman, 2023, p. 1)

The same organisation is doing work on a global basis encouraging the uptake of a second radical reframing of work through the Four Day Week initiative, where the standard working week is reduced from five to four days. They recently reported positive results from a UK pilot of this initiative that involved 61 companies and 2900 workers, which led to the following conclusions:

> With "before-and-after" data for a wide range of metrics, we have been able to measure the beneficial impact of a four-day week "across the board". Focusing on the narrow, "business case", for instance, we found that revenue stayed approximately the same (rising slightly by 1.4% over the trial), and was up 35% in comparison to the same period in 2021, while there were also improvements in hiring, absenteeism and resignations. Looking more broadly however, it is also clear that employees found themselves in a much improved position at the close of the trial than they did when it commenced. Shorter working hours left them less stressed and burned out, with their feedback also suggesting improved mental and physical health – perhaps not surprising given their increased time exercising and lower levels of fatigue. *As a result of the four-day week many employees therefore reported that their life satisfaction had improved.*
>
> (Lewis et al., 2023, pp. 67–68) [Emphasis added]

After Personal and Activist Time, we need to think carefully and deeply about a third and final framing of time, *Leadership Time*. This is in relation to our experiences alongside others and the environments we create for them when we are seen to occupy positions of authority at work. If your presence shapes the way those around you experience corporate life, how could you turn up differently to make the world of work more engaging and satisfying for them?

In considering the challenges that an existentialist approach brings to the leadership in business settings, it has been suggested that issues such as relatedness, meaning-making, values and beliefs, navigating uncertainty, authenticity, freedom, and emotional being are firmly to the fore (Hanaway, 2020, pp. 25–39). Additionally, the issue of temporality is also raised, with the following observation:

> We cannot control time, and concerns about control and temporality are evident throughout business practice. Our desire to transcend and control death and our knowledge that this is not possible leads us to seek control over what we believe we can control. Leadership offers itself as a piece in this existential puzzle.
>
> (Hanaway, 2020, p. 29)

This is why leadership is seen to be so significant these days both for those who lead and those who are deemed to be 'followers'. This fixation on leadership and work and the assumptions about what it is capable of in that context may be an indication of bad faith, as it draws us away from acknowledging and addressing our finitude (Hanaway, 2020, p. 29).

In light of this, a leader must be alert to how they are experiencing being in the role of leader, a concept that carries with it the dangers of essentialism given the volumes of published materials that aim to define what it is to be leader and what a leader should be seen to be doing. Some think of 'leader' as a *position*; others think of it as a *status*; in existential terms it is an invitation to become acutely aware of one's existence and to recognise that how you navigate what defines you as a person defines the experiences of those around you.

Bibliography

Aloisi, A., & De Stefano, V. (2022). Essential jobs, remote work and digital surveillance: Addressing the COVID-19 pandemic panopticon. *International Labour Review, 161*(2), 289–314.

Bakewell, S. (2016). *At the Existentialist Cafe: Freedom, Being & Apricot Cocktails*. London: Chatto & Windus.

Beal, J. (2025, January 3). Gen Z prefers 'employer for life' to 'job for life'. Retrieved 7 January 2025, from *The Times*: https://www.thetimes.com/uk/society/article/gen-z-prefers-employer-for-life-to-job-for-life-snc9z3fp3

Butler, J. (2009). Performativity, precarity, and sexual policies. *AIBR, Revista de antropología Iberoamericana*, 4(3), 321–336. Retrieved 7 January 2025, from https://revista.aibr.org/12

Camus, A. (1955/1991). *The Myth of Sisyphus and Other Essays*. New York: Vintage International.

Cavanaugh, R. (2024). The Master of the Absurd. In P. Now, *The Ultimate Guide to Existentialism* (pp. 111–113). London: Anja Publications Ltd.

Church of England. (2024, 11 December). *At the Burial of the Dead*. Retrieved 11 December 2024, from Church of England – The Book of Common Prayer https://www.churchofengland.org/prayer-and-worship/worship-texts-and-resources/book-common-prayer/burial-dead#na

Cole, M. (2020). *Radical Organisation Development*. Abingdon: Routledge.

Cole, M., & Higgins, J. (2022). *Leadership Unravelled: The Faulty Thinking behind Modern Management*. Abingdon: Routledge.

Cole, M., & Higgins, J. (2023). *The Great Unheard at Work: Understanging Voice and Silence in Organisations*. Abingdon: Routledge.

Day, R. (Director). (1961). *The Rebel* [Motion Picture]. Retrieved from https://en.wikipedia.org/wiki/The_Rebel_(1961_film)

Feifel, H. (1969). Death – relevant variable in psychology. In R. May (ed.), *Existential Psychology* (pp. 58–71). New York: Random House.

Frankl, V. E. (1946/2004). *Man's Search for Meaning: The Classic Tribute to Hope from the Holocaust*. London: Rider.

Frayne, D., & Goodman, C. (2023). *How Do We Pay for It? A Beginner's Guide to Basic Income Costings*. Retrieved 10 January 2025, from Autonomy https://actionnetwork.org/user_files/user_files/000/100/272/original/A_beginner%E2%80%99s_guide_to_basic_income_costings_-_Briefing.pdf

Graeber, D. (2019). *Bullshit Jobs: The Rise of Pointless Work and What We Can Do About It*. London: Penguin.

Hanaway, M. (2020). *An Existential Approach to Leadership Challenges*. Abingdon: Routledge.

IWGB. (2025). *Our History*. Retrieved 15 January 2025, from IWGB https://iwgb.org.uk/en/page/history

Komisar, R. (2001). *The Monk and the Riddle: The Art of Creating a Life while Making a Living*. Boston, MA: Harvard Business School Press.

Lefebvre, H. (1966). Theoretical problems of autogestion. In H. Lefebvre, N. Brenner, & S. Elden (Eds.), *State, Space, World: Selected Essays* (pp. 138–152). Minneapolis: University of Minnesota Press.

Lewis, K., Stronge, W., Kellam, J., & Kikuchi, L. (2023). *The Results are In: The UK's Four Day Week Pilot*. Crookham Village, Hants: Autonomy.

Martineau, J. (2016). *Time, Capitalism and Alienation: A Socio-Historical Inquiry into the Making of Modern Time*. Chicago: Haymarket.

Mateescu, A., & Nguyen, A. (2019). *Algorithmic Management in the Workplace*. New York City: Data & Society Research Institute.

Newsome, K., Heyes, J., Moore, S., Smith, D., & Tomlinson, M. (2018). *Living on the Edge: Experiencing Workplace Insecurity in the UK*. London: Trades Union Congress. Retrieved 30 January 2025, from https://www.tuc.org.uk/sites/default/files/insecure%20work%20report%20final%20final.pdf

Però, D. (2020). Indie Unions, organizing and labour renewal: Learning from precarious migrant workers. *Work, Employment and Society, 34*(5), 900–918.

Pontefract, D. (2024, September 28). *Conscious unbossing: why gen z is steering clear of middle management*. Retrieved 8 January 2025, from Forbes https://www.forbes.com/sites/danpontefract/2024/09/28/conscious-unbossing-why-gen-z-is-steering-clear-of-middle-management

Pósch, K., Cockbain, E., Beadsworth, J., Scott, S., Mantouvalou, V., & Bradford, B. (2024). *Measuring the Scale and Nature of Labour Market Noncompliance Affecting People in precarious Work in the UK: First Project Report*.

London: UCL Consultants Ltd. Retrieved 7 January 2025, from https://www.gov.uk/government/publications/assessment-of-the-scale-and-nature-of-labour-market-non-compliance-in-the-uk-interim-report

Reitz, M., & Higgins, J. (2025). *Permisson to Pause: Rediscovering 'Spaciousness' at Work.* Retrieved from Megan Reitz: https://static1.squarespace.com/static/597729cbcf81e0f87c7f6c61/t/677b9b9a26a22a7351dce717/1736154022120/SpaciousnessREPORT_90pp_FULL.pdf

Ronan, S. (2022, January 12). Boomers, millennials, Gen Z: Do generational labels do more harm than good? Retrieved 7 January 2025, from *HR Magazine* https://www.hrmagazine.co.uk/content/features/boomers-millennials-gen-z-do-generational-labels-do-more-harm-than-good/#:~:text=An%20open%20letter%20to%20the,on%20when%20they%20were%20born.

Sartre, J.-P. (2020). *Nausea.* London: Penguin Classics.

Vitak, J., & Zimmer, M. (2023). Surveillance and the future of work: Exploring employees' attitudes toward monitoring in a post-COVID workplace. *Journal of Computer-Mediated Communication, 28*(4), 1–12. Retrieved from https://academic.oup.com/jcmc/article/28/4/zmad007/7210235

Western, S. (2023). Covid - An intrusion of the real. In H. Brunning, & O. Khaleelee, *The Covid Trail: Psychodynamic Explorations* (pp. 139–156). Bicester: Phoenix Publishing House Ltd.

Westfall, C. (2025, 4 January). *The End of Management? Gen Z Faces New Challenges in 2025.* Retrieved 8 January 2025, from Forbes https://www.forbes.com/sites/chriswestfall/2025/01/03/the-end-of-management-gen-z-faces-new-challenges-in-2025

Wolff, J., & Leopold, D. (2021). *Karl Marx.* Retrieved 15 January 2025, from *The Stanford Encyclopedia of Philosophy* https://plato.stanford.edu/archives/spr2021/entries/marx

Zand, D. (2024, December 23). *Young people are rejecting work. Why?* Retrieved 6 January 2025, from *Financial Times* https://www.ft.com/content/609d3829-30db-4356-bc0e-04ba6ccfa5ed

4 Deriving meaning from work

Multiple meanings

I arrived at a point in my career just before I made the choice to accept a settlement and leave my salaried working life where I was finding myself being more and more challenging of the imposed norms that shape and direct the workplace. As I gingerly dipped my toe back into the brackish waters of the labour market thereafter, one thing that increasingly antagonised me was being asked at interview about the glib set of wearisome corporate values that sat in the shadows of the company to which I was applying for a role – and the extent to which my past practice resounded with those.

I knew what I was meant to say: I was expected to demonstrate a knowledge of a set of values to which I could not be said to have any meaningful allegiance, insofar as they belonged to an organisation that I was trying to join not of which I was already part. It is absurd to expect a candidate to retrospectively give an account of past experience in respect to values to which that individual has no meaningful connection.

Moreover, I had reached the conclusion – and had articulated this publicly in a number of published items – that by and large sets of corporate values were meaningless other than to the senior leadership of a corporation, where they could be said to bring together that fractionated peak of the organisation. The only way in which you can get Finance, HR, operations, and so on to collaborate rather than jostle against one another for position – and to prevent those people from stabbing the Chief Executive in the back – is to use values to lash them into position (Cole & Higgins, 2022, pp. 135–138).

DOI: 10.4324/9781003592624-4

Like a bad student sitting an exam, I chose several times to flip the question; instead of waffling on about whatever set of words or phrases the particular company to which I was applying had confected and announced as 'values', I offered the panel the opportunity to hear about my particular personal and professional beliefs and orientations that motivated me to work – and drew me to this particular job – and which prompted me to always seek to do the very best that I could.

It probably goes without saying that this did not land well in the formalised interview process, which is constructed in a way that is akin to a catechism: the employers chime a set of formulaic questions and the applicant provides them at each stage with the expected response, as opposed to an honest account of themselves in regard to a specific corporate topic. Ultimately, it is a deeply dishonest call-and-response, not because the people involved on either side are innately unethical but because the structure reproduces itself again and again … and, in so doing, constricts the room for fresh thinking and creative new approaches.

Whose meaning matters

As I attended these interviews, it became increasingly clear to me that these values were not simply explicit stipulations as to how I was meant to think and behave in this workplace. Instead, I recognised that each value – and the overall array of all of those corporate insistences – were actually meanings derived from the specific circumstances but arising out of the existence of others rather than appearing in light of my experience of working life. Hence, this increasingly became to my mind interpretations of the world that did not necessarily resonate with me – or, indeed, motivate me.

This came as an important reminder to me that the workplace is written through with a large number of meanings, some of which can be identified as dominant and actively imposed, whilst others are decidedly subaltern (Spivak, 1988). Corporate values are just one interpretation of meaning in organisational life. Whilst an exercise might have been undertaken through which to engage with staff members and customers in order – in principle – to generate these supposed defining statements, ultimately the ownership and promotion of a schedule of values sits very firmly at the top of any organisation.

People are mindful these days that power exists in the realm of the state in a liberal democracy (or, indeed, a dictatorship) but also increasingly this is mirrored by its presence in large corporate settings. This can be understood through a taxonomy of three types of power in organisational life: first, there is a *behavioural model*, wherein tension and conflict can be found to exist amongst individuals and groups in this setting and power is a resource that supports manipulation or coercion (Hiley, 1987).

Second, we are confronted by an *ideological model*, which can be usefully described as follows:

> Power is understood to operate not through explicit decision-making or the direct and overt influence of one person or group over another, but through the way a belief system or set of values figures in structuring or fostering the conditions for certain explicit outcomes – by producing the conditions for some outcomes and repressing the possibility of others; through latent conflicts, and through the prevention of certain interests or conflicts from surfacing for explicit consideration. Whereas the behavioral model focuses on the intentions of social actors, the ideological model focuses on structural factors within a system of beliefs or values.
>
> (Hiley, 1987, p. 345)

Lastly, the author draws heavily on the work of Michel Foucault in order to describe a third modality of power in the company setting, namely the *disciplinary model*. This focuses on power not as an instrument in the hands of someone or a group enjoying a particular structural position or indeed as an explicit set of beliefs and values that shapes the organisational infrastructure. Instead, it is a view of power that recognises that it emerges as a characteristic of any human-to-human interrelationship … and is woven deeply into the fabric of any social circumstance wherein people come together (Hiley, 1987). In most instances, it is unspoken and subtle, hidden away in the back and forth of corporate life … and present in all manner of elements, including, for example, corporate architecture, the deployment of space and time in organisational settings, and the construction of the whole range of company documents.

The meanings that exist in the firms in which we work are both ideological and also reflective of the more subtle modality of power that Foucault identifies. Tumbling down from the upper reaches of most companies come the intangible and alienated things like values that senior leaders feel obliged to focus upon and to invest energy in. There is an opportunity cost here, as it sees them consumed by this instead of turning their attention to what's going on in their organisations and what the people who work there are experiencing on a day-by-day basis. As we sit in the workplace finding ways to get done the tasks that we are charged to do in a hierarchy built largely on a monetary exchange, various ideological elements flutter down into the space that we occupy.

Corporate meanings

The visions, missions, and values that descend in this *meaning blizzard* have extremely limited impact on how we get our work done, so they do not feel immediately impactful as we sit doing what we are asked to do. However, they create ideological drifts of meaning that subtly reshape the terrain in which we work and determine how we see, think about, and engage with the overall environment. And they seep into the fabric of the workplace and reshape that in a way that goes largely unnoticed, although these subtle adjustments are absorbed by us in the course of our work life, and our thinking and practice is changed by them.

There is, of course, a strongly held view in the world of management that these activities are extremely impactful in terms of how companies work and how successful they are. In considering the linked practices of creating vision and drafting missions, for instance, it is argued that

> Vision is an idealistic projection of the company in an undefined future, in a mature and successful position. Vision is not a dream and not a fantasy. It is an idealistic projection of what the company might be and might achieve.
>
> (Brătianu & Bălănescu, 2008, p. 20)

In a world where so much is patently both uncertain and unknowable, such an assertion appears extremely hubristic. Philosophically, one wonders what the presumed benefit might be in practical terms to craft a picture of one's company in a future that is patently too complex for any human being to claim to be able to forecast. It may not be, as the authors aver, a dream or a fantasy ... but it would very much look to be a confabulated fiction. It is a fuzzy image sitting somewhere in an even fuzzier landscape ... so cannot be said to serve a practical purpose in terms of crafting the company or shaping the future, practices that uncertainty put beyond the grasp of any human agent. Instead, it acts solely as a condensation of meaning arising from a specific elevated perspective, namely the boardroom, that acts not as a guide but as a constraint on those who find themselves in the midst of it. Meanings that we might derive from our corporate existence are denied by this dominant – and domineering – set of views.

Having a sense of intention seems eminently more grounded in the way in which we actually experience existence than does the idea of crafting and pursuing a plan. In corporate contexts, this notion is left looking all the more absurd by the fact that the concrete practice of business planning seeks to create an immutable picture of how and when things will be achieved. This fails to acknowledge that existence – for both human agents and for the organisations that they create or find themselves joining – is a moment-by-moment thing. We have the power to choose, but there is then a clear sense that each action on our part and on the part of those around us will impact and shift the immediate reality through which we are seeking to make our way.

In considering the second element of managerial meaning-making it is suggested that:

> Mission reflects the way in which vision can be transformed into a tangible existence for the company. Looking at the mission statement from a more practical view, we may say that it is more realistic than the company's vision, answering the following questions: who, what and why. WHO we are? WHAT we want to create? WHY we want to exist? All possible answers cluster around the consumer needs, stakeholders interests, shareholders financial returns, and our legacy to create value and competitive advantage.
>
> (Brătianu & Bălănescu, 2008, p. 21)

Ultimately, both vision and mission are constructed meanings, written through with power in light of where they tend to originate in the business world and the seniority of the people who take control of these in reality quite ethereal and yet culturally influential elements. The dominance of these meanings deny space and opportunity for alternative and subordinate meanings to emerge and give shape to the corporate context. Indeed, a seminal work in this regard quite explicitly pursues the notion that the personal presence and practice of the senior leadership expressly and exclusively determines the nature of the company. The thesis that they seek to evidence is built around the following perspective: 'Organizational outcomes – both strategies and effectiveness – are viewed as reflections of the values and cognitive bases of powerful actors in the organizations. (Hambrick & Mason, 1984, p. 193). It will certainly realise one version of the outcomes. However, refusing the voice of others within an organisation prevents the emergence of alternative views of what outcome actually means in this context.

Elsewhere, a causal link between the values specifically of the Chief Executive, the culture of the organisation that they seek to lead, and the outcomes of that company is made is observed (Berson et al., 2008). In focusing on the impact of those in the boardroom, this approach ends up privileging the meaning that this select band of individuals impose upon their workplaces – and leads to the notion of Core Group Theory, an analysis of corporate life that identifies the elite coalitions who drive organisations forward and whose needs and expectations define what the organisation does and how it does it (Kleiner, 2003).

Of even greater concern is that the normalising effect of focusing on just these senior people means that those below them, who might well take a distinctly different view of the world of work in which they find themselves, are cast as running against the corporate normalcy that is generated by the imposition of the managerialist meaning … and that the Othering effect reinforces the silencing that people at the base of the hierarchy experience.

It is worth taking a moment to articulate what this term means, in respect to its derivation from the work of poststructuralist writers such as Foucault and Lacan:

> Othering is defined as a process in which, through discursive practices, different subjects are formed, hegemonic subjects – that is, subjects in powerful social positions as well as those subjugated to these powerful conditions. To arrive at such an analytic description, however, some measure of abstraction is required, because Othering denotes simultaneously both the features of discourse structures and processes, and the formation of subjectivity engendered by such discourse.
>
> (Thomas-Olalde & Velho, 2011, p. 27)

In the discussions surrounding this conceptualisation highlighting the interrelationship between notions of normalcy and the Othering that occurs as a result of that, there is a strong suggestion that this effect is extremely noticeable in 'cultures that continuously, routinely, comprehensively, and institutionally make themselves statistically transparent' (Link, 2004, p. 18). The presence of a dominant – and domineering – meaning (or set of linked meanings) creates a vision of normality, so that – should anyone contest it or look to find ways in which to offer a different view of the world – they will find themselves pushed to the periphery, defined negatively in contrast to the prevailing view.

Dominant meanings

At the time of drafting this chapter, two news stories came to my attention that seemed in many ways to reinforce these observations about meaning in the workplace. The first involved someone called James Watt, one of the co-founders of the BrewDog beer company. As ever in such instances in a capitalist society, it is extremely difficult to establish how hard this individual had to work to get his company started in contrast to how hard others had to work for him and under his management to make his corporate dream a reality. It would appear that most of his time is spent now in the company of his partner, someone who appeared in the public domain as a result of reality TV and who now distinguishes herself with the vacuous description of social media influencer.

In that regard, it is reported that the couple publicly shared a video which focused on a key complaint: it was argued that the UK lacks a work orientation, which presumably can be translated to mean that people object to slaving away so that someone like Watt can get rich and inflict their half-baked opinions on the world. In a *Times* article about this episode – which apparently led to him receiving death threats via his medium of choice – Watt is quoted as saying that 'The whole concept of work-life balance was invented by people who hate what they do' (Hughes, 2025) What seems particularly offensive about his intervention, if the article is accurate in this regard, is that he stepped down from his role at the brewer in 2024 after 17 years and that 'When he announced his departure, Watt said that he planned to take time off, travel and spend more time with family and friends' (Hughes, 2025).

This looks to be a supreme example of that parental instruction that states, 'Don't do as I do, do as I tell you'. But, more importantly, it feels like a powerful reminder that work is something that we are not simply compelled to do in order to exist in the work lives into which we find ourselves thrown but that we are also expected to embrace with boundless enthusiasm. The meaning imposed on us in this news story derives from someone who has spent a lot of their career at the top of an organisation – and it is so harshly expressed as to completely *Other* us if we are seen to take a position where we look to craft a meaning out of our existence that focuses on the importance to us of life above and beyond the all too familiar corporate constraints.

The second insight into how meaning in our company contexts tends to derive directly from those at the top of the firm comes from an item in the *Financial Times* that talks about the chair of Larsen & Toubro, an Indian multinational corporation, who had been caught at an internal 'town hall' meeting saying that he wished he could compel all of his employees to work 90 hours a week. S. N. Subrahmanyan was reported as saying, '"If I could make you work on Sundays, I would be more happy because I work on Sundays also." "What do you do sitting at home?" he added. "How long can you stare at your wife, how long can the wife stare at her husband? Come on, get to the office and start working"' (Reed, 2025).

This intervention became especially newsworthy because, as the article suggested, it highlighted what are described as 'twin obsessions of the country's professional class: long work hours and their toll on family life' (Reed, 2025). This offers insight into what can be said to be meant by meaning in respect to life, with a clear indication of how one person's meaning – particularly that of somebody occupying the upper echelons of a hierarchy – can be felt to be normal and hence imposable on others. Because Subrahmanyan has chosen a life in which he opts to work on Sundays, his bad faith appears where, rather than changing his own life, he seeks to impose the misery of his own experience on others.

Additionally, to parse his remarks a little further, he chooses to belittle domestic life in a decidedly peculiar fashion, suggesting that – instead of working – spouses are merely sitting at home and staring at one another. Again, Subrahmanyan evidently privileges a life that is dominated by work; in elevating this to its paramount position, he relegates ways in which others might choose to balance their existence by making sneering remarks about one possibility. He denigrates what could – to some – be argued to be a vision of domestic contentment and connection.

All of which underscores the fact that finding meaning in life is a vital existentialist orientation – and one that resides at the core of how we might choose to live our lives. On his blog called *Leadership Freak*, Dan Rockwell pithily summarises this in a way that nudges his reader to actively embrace their own responsibility for purpose at work:

> Your boss can't give you meaning. Neither can your organization. You can work in healthcare and feel work is meaningless. You can work on an assembly line and find meaning in monotonous work. Meaning doesn't come from delivering babies or peeling potatoes. Meaning comes from within. Activities can be useful or destructive, moral or immoral, difficult or easy, energizing or monotonous. We don't find meaning at work. We bring meaning to work.
>
> (Rockwell, 2024)

Making meaning

As noted, organisations would benefit hugely from paying attention to the values that bring people to their door in the hope of working for their company and doing the best job that they possibly can. This would be far better than doing what currently happens most of the time, which is crudely trying to impose a set of corporate values that they conjured out of nothing. Encouraging people explicitly to find meaning in their work and engaging with the perspectives that they personally create would be hugely useful for all concerned.

On one occasion, an organisation at which I worked was so short of staff that we actively recruited almost an entire cohort of students who were just graduating as newly qualified health-care professionals. Those of us involved in this exercise worked hard to ensure that a comprehensive preceptorship arrangement was in place over time for these new starters. On reflection, though, I realise that I missed a trick in respect to this cadre of fresh staff members in two respects: first, I signally failed to follow up with them as they arrived to ask them what they were seeing as they joined the workplace … and to what extent did they feel reassured or concerned about the thinking, processes, procedures, and practices into which they found themselves cast. Their 'thrownness' into a particular workplace situation was something that they experienced – and which I could have asked them about, in order to get a richer picture of the workplace in which I had perhaps become too familiar.

Linked to this was a failure to acknowledge that these individuals who had just completed their training at a university were likely to have an extremely up-to-date understanding of how things were expected to be done in the contemporary health-care setting. The failure to explore this reinforces the idea that the business of recruitment is more about corporate absorption – follow our values; fit in with how things are and don't rock the boat; focus on doing what is demanded of you instead of speaking up in regard to ways in which things might be improved – than actively engaging with talent. This resonates with the largely unsubstantiated suggestion that 'Henry Ford even once lamented, "Why is it that every time I ask for a pair of hands, they come with a brain attached?" Critical thinking, creativity, and individual agency were irrelevant to the business. A nuisance. Factories could be run by robots — if they existed' (Suarez-Battan, 2021).

This suggests that I was complicit with a way of being that prioritised one sense of meaning – the corporate narrative – and actively neglected the meanings that everyone – including, of course, me – brought to work with them and developed in the course of their employment, but kept silent about. But, perhaps more importantly, the argument is advanced that ultimately creating meaning for ourselves is a way to give substance to our lives – instead of simply lapsing into the Camusian notion that human life is merely absurd – and this is a crucial factor in allowing us a sense of contentment and engagement with life.

It is meaning, then, that gives us the strength to confront life, notwithstanding how it might be in our experience. As Viktor Frankl argues from bitter experience of the Hitler regime,

> There is nothing in the world, I venture to say, that would so effectively help me to survive even the worst conditions as the knowledge

> that there is a meaning in one's life. There is much wisdom in the words of Nietzsche: "He who has a why to live can bear almost any how." … In the Nazi concentration camps, one could have witnessed that those who knew that there was a task waiting for them to fulfill were most apt to survive.
>
> (Frankl, 1946/2004, p. 109)

This perspective on meaning renders it equivalent to the notion of purpose, whereas – in an existentialist sense – it can be seen to draw from Sartre's argument that existence precedes essence, which atheistically can be taken to mean that 'first of all, man exists, turns up, appears on the scene, and, only afterwards, defines himself … Man is nothing else but what he makes of himself' (Sartre, 1957/1985, p. 15). Removing God from the equation of life, as Sartre and others such as Heidegger do, means that defining ourselves resides exclusively with us, not as an abstract notion but in the course of the thoughts and choices we make in the moment as we live our lives.

Absenting a deity means that there is no omniscient being whose ascribed values will provide us with a model of how to live … and, because God is not there to see us, there is no human nature defined by his knowing of us. However, it might then be argued that we then tend to deify those above us in the hierarchies that we inhabit in the workplace.

This doubles down on what we face in terms of choosing how we live: morality becomes entirely of our own making, and – at the same time – there is no secular definition of what our nature is seen to be as human beings. To embrace this responsibility requires us to acknowledge and enact the key observation that 'Human beings are meaning-making machines. It is our natural instinct to try and make sense of what we experience' (Jacob, 2019). Even those with faith in their lives might be said to fall within this definition, especially those for whom their theology is an ongoing debate about God's presence and what it means to live in that context as a human agent. All of which means that 'Life has only the meaning you choose to give it' (Cox, 2014, p. 113).

Existentialist engagement

For some, the notion of a morality separate from faith and religiosity is seen as something that is not easily achievable, if indeed at all possible. Specifically, if human beings are cut adrift and left to define how they wish to be in the world without reference to some other external metanarrative, the vision arises of myriad individuals making their way in their lives exactly as they choose. In respect to this calculation of what is right to do and whether this means that I shall do it, one relevant discussion in ethical philosophy is usefully explored by David Hume, who himself explains:

> [A]ccording to the imperfect way in which human affairs are conducted, a *sensible knave*, in particular incidents, may think, that an act of iniquity or infidelity will make a considerable addition to his fortune, without causing any considerable breach in the social union and confederacy. That *honesty is the best policy*, may be a good general rule; but is liable to many exceptions: And he, it may, perhaps, be thought, conducts himself with most wisdom, who observes the general rule, and takes advantage of all the exceptions.
>
> (Hume, 1777/1912, p. 122) [Emphasis in original]

It occurs to me that one aftermath of the Covid crisis has been more and more people embracing the role of the so-called sensible knave. This extends beyond those people who rejected the constraints that were introduced as governments struggled with the evidence as it developed to find logical ways in which to try and prevent the spread of the disease, given the potential if a significant number of people became contagiously sick with the virus for the economy upon which society depended to falter and for the health-care system to be overwhelmed by the unwell. Such a combination suggested a possibility for the veneer of civilisation to promptly fall away and leave us all as knaves, potentially having to leave aside the notion of cleaving to sense and rationality in order to protect ourselves and those dear to us as we moved from control to chaos.

More recently, I find myself personally aware of a greater sense of antisocial incivility. Where people come together in shared environments, such as supermarkets, it strikes me that a fresh sense of 'me, me, me' prevails and levels of politeness have been eroded by a crude assertion of the individual and their right to be as they choose, regardless of those around them. Something similar it seems to me can be seen on our roads, where reckless speeding and driving styles that seem to make a virtue of failing to acknowledge that there are other road users appear to prevail in way too many instances.

If my interpretation has a grounding in reality– and I may be merely projecting things onto life around me – it strikes me as unsurprising. I often tell the story of a mental health nurse who I was able to see during a particular period of crisis for me late in the Covid pandemic and to whom I spoke about feeling consumed by an overbearing sense of morbidity who smiled gently and replied, 'Well, that's not surprising, to be fair. We've spent two years with the government talking constantly and pretty much exclusively about death.' In the previous chapter, I made the observation that, as human beings, we tend to work to avoid being confronted by our own finitude: we distract ourselves by immersing ourselves in pursuits that require a high degree of busyness – including, of course, the job that we do and the workplace in which we do it – and mentally ensure that we are in denial of this critical fact of the limit to life.

Regarding that denial of temporality, it is here we find that cabal of plutocrats who dominate the world in terms of their companies and their wealth, shovelling money into research to reverse ageing and extend life. Chief among these, apparently, is Peter Thiel, a Silicon Valley businessperson with a strong interest in politics of a powerfully libertarian bent. His view of the world, apparently, is heavily informed by a neo-liberal tract co-authored by James Dale Davidson and William Rees-Mogg, the latter being the inky-fingered journalist who became editor of *The Times* in the UK and was father to Jacob Rees-Mogg. This publication is built on a conservative ideology of the individual that refutes any sense of collectivity, up to and including developments such as the nation state and its supra-national manifestations (Davidson & Rees-Mogg, 1997).

It was Thiel – amongst others – who became transfixed by what he perceived to be the imminent arrival of a global apocalypse a few years ago, which saw him use his wealth and reputation to seek an isolated place to live in New Zealand, so as to evade the effects of this destructive event – and, perhaps more importantly, escape the taxation demands of the state of California (O'Connell, 2018). A report in *The Guardian* newspaper highlighted the way in which capitalist oligarchs like Thiel and Bezos were busily ploughing money into companies such as Altos Labs to support research into halting – and possibly reversing – the ageing process – and reported that 'Thiel has claimed it will be possible to "reverse all human ailments in the same way that we can fix the bugs of a computer program. Death will eventually be reduced from a mystery to a solvable problem"' (Sample, 2022).

Here we see a prime example of people acting in bad faith: instead of focusing on how best to live the life into which they are thrown, these individuals distract themselves with the fantastic notion that, in some fashion, by combining scientific method with boundless resources, it is within their grasp to put an end to temporality. The supreme irony here is that someone like Jeff Bezos – a key funder of Altos Labs – is responsible for a global IT company that fills the world with 'stuff'. When John Higgins and I visited an Amazon fulfilment centre to acquire some insight into what this modern-day workplace looked and felt like, I was immediately taken by the fact that the depot was packed to the gunnels with goods.

The IT system that oversaw these structures allocated items to vacant space on the shelves rather than organising that storage on the basis of categories, so a single cursory glance revealed ridiculous juxtapositions in one small section of shelving, such as the presence of plastic straws, children's dolls, and a cleaning product, all in one place. While Bezos actively seeks to find ways in which to prolong his life, he earns the money that supports that research by potentially filling the world with more and more material – and thence quite likely making it less habitable in the long run for those who can afford to extend their existence.

Beyond the immediately recognisable names of Big Tech, we find other grotesquely wealthy individuals engaged in weird pursuits that seek to deny the actuality of being alive in the world. For example, it is reported that

> Tech millionaire Bryan Johnson has been injected with his 17-year-old son's plasma in a quest to reverse the ageing process and attain the body of an 18-year-old. Johnson previously hit headlines for revealing he was spending $2 million (£1.6 million) a year on an intense regime to reduce his biological age.
>
> (Morris, 2023)

In the same article, Johnson was reported as having claimed that – as a result of his investment in an anti-ageing research company – he had a chronological age of 44 but a biological age of 36.

Interestingly, other than the somewhat vampiric pursuit of the blood of his offspring, the regime to which he ascribes the fact that he is ageing slower than the average 10-year-old actually involves: a healthy diet, portion control and some fasting; an extensive number of supplements taken daily; and a hefty exercise regime. This calls to mind the old joke that such a regimen won't necessarily make you live longer, although it will bloody well feel like it!

Existential ethics

Aside from a handful of high-profile people trying to use their wealth to deny how life is lived in our eco-system, we all of us need to embrace the idea that meaning arises out of us rather than from somewhere outside of our existence. For many of us who have no religion or faith, we find ourselves trying to navigate our lives in a place where meaning is wholly absent – and has never been present. It is difficult to deny the anguish that accompanies this description of how we find ourselves in the world:

> We really have no grip on why the universe is here at all. It is irrational. It might all be snuffed out in the next instant for all we know. And yet we go on, carving whatever meaning we can into this silent world. Of course, this leads many to nihilism or hedonism: if there's no sense or meaning in the world, then why live in any other way than doing just what feels right to you? This is certainly rampant in the world right now.
>
> (Rickles, 2022, p. 22)

Instead of lapsing into an entirely meaningless view of the world as utterly absurd or embracing an amoral commitment to do whatever one wants because nothing actually matters, Rickles urges us to embrace a more positive outlook that acknowledges death as a compass by which we might navigate the choppy waters of existence. He argues that finitude in this sense compels us to actively decide in terms of making our choices because the alternative is that 'Unlimited time would imply that all possible outcomes could occur at some point, so that choice would not even be a coherent concept – it would simply *dissolve into the boundless*' (Rickles, 2022, p. xiii) [Emphasis in original]. A salutary reminder to those of whom we have spoken who seek to find ways to defy death.

The meaning of work

All of this leads to a tentative conclusion that our experience of work is shaped by a constantly changing number of meanings, most of which derive from someone else and are heard the loudest in the context of paid employment because of the positional power that allows those voices to be dominant.

Some amongst us may well find meaning through the work that we end up doing in this context; that said, though, we need to recall that, from an existentialist point of view, doing that work and finding meaning in it could be seen as an act of bad faith, because – in deriving satisfaction from the superficiality of daily work – we are conveniently avoiding asking ourselves:

> Why am I spending what little time I have here in pursuit of this particular endeavour, given how time-consuming it is?

> Is investing myself in the work that I find myself being asked to do – or that I choose for myself to do – the way in which I truly wish to live my life ... and, if so, why? And – if not – what would I prefer to choose to do?

In practical terms, there is an argument for trying to find a way through which to create deeply personal meaning out of our immersion in the world of work. If the socio-economic facticity says that we are unavoidably cast as wage-slaves and that the act of refuting the extant way of being in terms of our relationship to work is unobtainable in current circumstances, then it is especially important that we are reflexively engaged with this key aspect of our life ... and that we assert ourselves within limits so as to allow ourselves to create a rich meaning from our presence at work, while negotiating the fragile boundary between our life at large and our working life.

As we have seen, the Sartrean notion of meaning-making puts the human agent very much in the driving seat, which was touched upon earlier but is more fully described thus:

> [F]irst of all, man exists, turns up, appears on the scene, and, only afterwards, defines himself. If man, as the existentialist conceives him, is indefinable, it is because at first he is nothing. Only afterward will he be something, and he himself will have made what he will be ... Not only is man what he conceives himself to be, but he is also only what he wills himself to be after this thrust toward existence.
>
> (Sartre, 1957/1985, p. 15)

This means that we build ourselves from scratch – and do so without template or model, in terms of both the history that precedes our appearance in the world and also the narratives that have arisen out of humankind that seek to offer explanation of life and a design to which we should shape ourselves. By way of further explanation, our existence can be conceptualised as the sudden appearance in the world of a slab of stone or a lump of clay, which starts to chisel and mould itself immediately, but with no image in mind as a draft of what statue or figurine we are trying to create. In terms of this notion of self-creation, there is a clear implication that we make meaning for ourselves and generate an overall sense of purpose. It is within this act of creation of ourselves that we discern the freedom and choice that existentialism puts at the heart of its thinking about being in the world.

The demand that we step forward to act instead of relying on extant ideas of being and what it means to be resonates with what Viktor Frankl refers to as the *existential vacuum*, a state wherein we experience deep feelings of meaninglessness, emptiness, futility, and frustration. As he goes on to explain,

> [I]n contrast to an animal, man is not told by drives and instincts what he simply *must* do. Furthermore, in contrast to man in former times, today he is no longer told by the traditions and traditionally and universally held values what he *should* do. Now neither knowing what he must do nor what he should do, he sometimes seems no longer to know what he basically *wishes* to do. And what is the consequence? Either he just wishes to do what other people are doing – this is *conformism*; or else he just does what other people wish him to do – and this is *totalitarianism*.
>
> (Frankl, 2024, p. 38) [Emphasis in original]

In their reading of Frankl's rich work, Monica Hanaway – in a useful volume that outlines details of the practice of existential coaching – emphasises three elements via which a person can make meaning in the world, namely: *creativity*, meaning what we give to the world in terms of thinking about and doing things; *experiencing*, which centres on our relationships with all manner of the external, including nature and culture; and *change of attitude*, where we confront something that we cannot personally change but where we can opt to adjust our attitude towards that experience. This is undergirded by the principle that we have a will to meaning … and that we are free to realise that will and to find meaning at all times (Hanaway, 2020b, p. 99).

Meanings made for me … and that I made

The challenge of freedom derives primarily from two sources: the need for us to make a meaningful personal commitment to act in good faith and follow through on the choices that we make; and the fact that we experience that freedom in a wider social context that actively limits it. In a social context, whilst we may find reasons to steer away from it, it is far easier for us to reject ideas and proposals offered to us than accept them. When I was at university, my friend Andrew christened me 'Mr Nope', as he would regularly make suggestions of things for us to do – and my terse and hurtful response was simply to dismiss it, invariably by just uttering the word 'No'. While sociability in most instances requires us to navigate an exchange such as this – one person offers an idea, the other finds a gentle way to express a lack of interest in it – with politeness and generosity at the forefront, not least so that the threads that connect us in person-to-person relationships do not become frayed by an abrasive reaction, it remains easier in this social setting to find our way to deny a request than to accept it.

The workplace, however, feels somewhat different, not least because it is invariably hierarchically stacked and is written through with largely unacknowledged power. This is why the vision of an organisation – deriving from those in its upper echelons and with little consideration of how this lands with all of the others in that company – is actually a dominant interpretation of the circumstances in which a large number of people find themselves. It is the meaning derived from immersion in the specific working context that is imposed on others – and hence either at best stifles the meanings that others might derive from their experience or actively mobilises power in a subterranean fashion so as to deny those people the chance to even consider developing an alternative meaning.

Throughout most of my working life, I am painfully aware these days that I largely surrendered to the idea that it would be others around me who would make sense of the context in which we all came together. I behaved in the way that Frankl suggested earlier: I did as others were doing and did as others told me. I conformed and succumbed to the control of others (even in instances where those people had not actively sought out that capacity to manage the context and me in it). I did not merely deny my own agency; I actively effaced that agency in response to the agency of others to whom I made one crucial choice, namely that I would follow their lead.

An example of creating room for my own meaning …

There are perhaps two exceptions to this across my 40 or so year career in the workplace: first, as an operating department orderly, while the work itself seemed difficult to derive meaning from given what we were expected to do and how we were treated when doing it, the people with whom I worked directly and our connections in the particular context of a certain type of work and our respective position in a hierarchical stack of occupational respect and management activity opened up a meaning that was experienced at a tangent to the main focus of my employment. I found meaning with the people *with* whom I worked … but certainly not from those *for* whom I worked.

Sitting at the bottom of the pile, we theatre porters – mere manual workers, whose task was to accompany a nurse to take a patient to and from the operating theatre … and also to move the patient and equipment about under instruction of those above us in the structure – were treated with utter disdain. I often tell the story of racing to change into scrubs in order to be available in a timely fashion to support the early start of an operating list. There were no grey scrubs, which was the colour that theatre porters were expected to wear; I could not find a blue set to wear, which was the clothing worn by nurses; but there were plenty of the surgeons' green scrubs available, so I changed into a set of those.

Seconds later, the theatre sister – a person who paid obeisance to the medical staff, exercised considerable control of the nurses, and could be seen to be deeply discomforted when she had to engage with six young men who, despite their structurally lowly status, often found the courage to contest ideas that others in her domain merely accepted as unchallengeable tradition – collared me as I went about the business of responding to the commands and requests of the other nurses as they endeavoured to get the work started. 'Why are you wearing green?' she demanded. I explained that no grey overalls had come back from the laundry. 'But the surgeons wear green', she countered. I was momentarily tickled by the notion that someone would mistake me for a member of the surgical team. In the end, she demanded that I went off to change, thereby reducing the portering workforce from six to five at one of the busiest times.

The meaning that arose out of this relationship between clothing coloured grey, blue, and green literally had nothing to do with me, although I was expected to comply with it without question. Indeed, the meaning I ascribed to the circumstances that I faced was completely different: I assumed that the priority should be that I was promptly available to do the job that was expected of me in terms of supporting a list of operations, which would mean getting dressed as quickly as possible in whatever scrubs were available for me. However, the dynamics of the circumstances in which I found myself placed a tight binding on me in terms of how I might engage with the world of work as an existential free agent. And the shape of the regime in which I existed offered no wriggle room wherein the dominant view could be contested, and my alternative view could be surfaced: in that sense, my voice was denied in terms of saying 'no' to a situation not of my making – and my silence was demanded in face of the perspective of those above me.

Another example of creating room for my own meaning …

To add an additional layer of complication to this, the experience of theatre porters that I have described here was how it felt to be in that role between the hours of 8am and 5pm. At the end of the day, five of the six porters got changed back into their normal clothes and disappeared for the night, leaving just one of us rostered as 'on-call'. This meant staying late if the operating list overran and also being available if an emergency needed to come to the theatre at some point between 5pm and 8am.

Magically, as the clock ticked past the end of the official working day, the porter went from being an unthinking stack of muscle, a programmable meat machine, expected to follow orders and do the menial tasks of moving things around in the operating suite, to a member of the team. Suddenly, from merely moving people and lights and oxygen cylinders, the on-call porter was opening sterile surgical packs; helping the surgeon and the nurses with their scrubbing up; and counting out instruments, sutures, and swabs. At this point, the engagement from my perspective was hugely enhanced and I started to feel as though I was genuinely contributing in an important way to a vital process. I felt a sense of meaning that, during the working day, was wholly absent.

Another instance of creating room for my own meaning …

This was the time when I was a trade union shop steward at the hospital. The lack of meaning that prevailed in my day-to-day experience of a working life shaped by the meaning that others ascribed to it paradoxically gave me a massive sense of meaning in terms of seeking to represent the workforce. I was connected to the world and seeking to creatively improve it for those who I looked to represent. All of which seems to suggest that an authentic life in existential terms arises out of actively contesting largely unchallenged dominant meanings while – at the same time – creatively seeking to articulate one's own meaning through – to borrow the triangle mentioned above – creativity, experience, and change of attitude.

The business of managing meaning

Back in 1971, an animated children's programme called *Mr Benn* arrived on our screens. It featured the eponymous character in a suit and bowler hat, looking to all intents and purposes like he was on his way to a job in the City of London. He left his home at 52 Festive Avenue and looked as though he was headed for the daily commute. Instead, he made his way to an uncanny fancy dress shop, run by an exotic looking character who appeared out of nowhere each time Mr Benn went into the seemingly empty store. On each occasion, our hero picked out a costume and disappeared into a changing room to try it on, a space that had a mysterious secret back door through which Mr Benn walked, only to find himself transported through time and space to a location in keeping with the outfit that he had chosen to wear on that day.

So much of our lives feels to be shaped by what I am moved to call the Mr Benn Effect. This begins with the assumption that there is one true self, an essentialist version of our personhood and a template to which we should constantly return. Very often in corporate contexts, we are invited to bring this (fictional) edition of ourselves to work. Importantly, this is where the respective business and existentialist definitions of authenticity stand in sharp contrast: the workplace fixates on the idea of the one true self, while existentialist philosophy highlights that it arises out of living a life that knowledgeably embraces freedom and choice.

In the same way that Mr Benn dons an outfit – a suit of armour, for example – and is magically transported to an entirely different context, so there is a strong sense for us all that we are constantly juggling a range of titles and roles in life, as if together they offer a *dramatis personae* of characters that we then perform in a theatrical vision of our life. At home, we may be seen to be partner, spouse, parent, and grandparent; in the workplace, we are seen as employee, workmate, manager, leader, and staff representative. Each of these roles is built on the notion that it describes an essence to which we must aspire. This has the potential for us to think of our existence as akin to Mr Benn's experience, stepping in and out of a range of archetypes and redefining ourselves with each persona into which we choose to step.

Instead, an existentialist perspective would be to focus on our presence in life. As an individual thrown into the world, we should home in on the constant in all of this, namely our existence – and the way in which our engagement with that world and the choices that we make are the things that define us as a person, rather that ascribing a definition to ourselves on the basis of the role that we feel that we are occupying at any given moment.

In a corporate context, this should lead us to eschew the idea of being a 'manager' or a 'leader' and encourage us to place our existence at the centre of how we think and what we do in life. Instead of aspiring to be a 'good manager' or a 'respected leader', we should focus on being a thoughtful human being, looking to find our way through the complexity of life – and mindful of the way in which our presence in the world impacts others. This underscores the fact that focusing on being what is seen to be a manager or a leader in business may lead us to behave in bad faith, as we chase an ideal instead of taking the deeply personal responsibility of living an honest and personally meaningful life, alongside others trying to find their way in the world. In practical terms, it is argued that:

> Existential leaders build their leadership approach around existential beliefs and concerns of uncertainty, authenticity, relatedness, freedom and meaning … The approach requires a deep awareness of and attention to the existential human givens – our need for self-esteem, the need to be heard, the importance of time and temporality, the core place of values and beliefs, the human requirement for meaning, our experience and dread of uncertainty and our emotional engagement with ourselves, others and the world.
>
> (Hanaway, 2020a, p. 25)

In terms of thinking about the titles in the workplace behind which we so often hide or are expected to embody, when I introduced an appraisal system across the organisation of which I was part that turned away from traditional performance management in favour of a more conversational approach that foregrounded coaching practice as a way of structuring those exchanges, I undertook that work as a head of learning and organisation development … or rather as a version of what that role was said to look like and how it was meant to function at work.

When it came to me – in the role of 'manager' – trying to run an appraisal session using this new approach with a person who worked brilliantly well in the department, I performed what I was expected to do – in terms of the things I had inflicted on others – but did not feel natural in terms of this experience. At the end of the session, I invited my colleague – in typical managerialist style – to feel free to share with me how she had felt about the meeting we had just had. She offered her personal opinions – but then very helpfully observed that I had looked uncomfortable throughout it, as if it was something that did not feel quite right for me as a person.

She had pointed out an important disparity: in my role as someone promoting this new way of working, I knew what I was expected to do and created an approximation of it in terms of how I conducted myself; but, as a human being, she had noted that I talked a lot about inviting the staff to come up with ideas and experiment with them … but actually her experience was that I came up with ideas, spent time on my own working them up, and tended thereafter to share them with others – with the expectation that they would take my ideas and merely deliver them in practice.

What's important to me in this story is that it is easier to make sense of (and to derive different ways of) being when one notes the titles behind which we are hiding … and thence to bring the 'Me' to the foreground. At root, I am finding myself confronted here with the idea that far too often in corporate life we notice ourselves (or, perhaps, in many instances, do not notice ourselves or spot it too late) doing something because that is the thing that a particular design of person, for example a manager, is expected to do.

From an existentialist perspective, this has the feel of 'I was only obeying orders', albeit ones that arise out of the variety of essences that humankind creates for itself to avoid confronting finitude and agency rather than an external authority. Equally, we can find ourselves rationalising the things we have done, having made the choice to appear to be a particular type of person in the workplace to evade too close an association between our existence and the things we have to deliver in that context. This feels to me – theoretically and on the basis of practical experiences in my own working life – to be similar in some fashion to the old school excuse that 'A big kid did it and ran away!'

Making meaning together

Detaching myself from the list of characters in which I can opt to secrete myself and live in bad faith by denying my agency is not at all easy. But living life is a moment-by-moment challenge when we opt to be actively aware of those conditions. Making being at work a more comfortable and meaningful experience for all of humankind demands an engagement with that work. It's easy to camouflage oneself with notions such as head of, director, and chief executive – and to relax into the sense that the decisions and actions flowing from that covering have nothing to do with us … but, in light of some abstract rationalism, simply have to happen, so unavoidably have to be done. This is an abdication of responsibility, something that existentialism takes to be especially problematic in terms of seeking to live our lives in a way that is aware.

It is also important to note that meaning can be said to derive from the particular constellation of positional presences in a company … and that, arising from people's unthinking occupation of these spaces, is the imposition of meaning on others and a denial of the meanings that could arise from below. This is an important reminder that existentialism has a strongly individual focus, one that puts the person and their express responsibility to the fore. Sartre struggled to reconcile the philosophy that he developed with the ideology to which he wanted to subscribe. In terms of rationalising this, we find him stating that "[W]e were convinced at the time that historical materialism furnished the only valid interpretation of history and that existentialism remained the only concrete approach to reality. I do not pretend to deny the contradictions in this attitude' (Sartre, 1963, p. 21).

Despite the attraction to Sartre of Marxism as a rationalisation of activism, it should perhaps be noted that 'Classes do not act in Sartre's eyes; at best they form milieus. In this way, Sartre implicitly contests the Marxist idea of a revolution by the proletariat' (Betschart, 2019, p. 79). If this interpretation feels correct, it seems akin to those instances where leading figures in Christian churches have expressed scepticism about the existence of God and have denigrated key epistemic aspects of the theology to which they notionally demonstrate an allegiance. In analysing Sartre's politics, it has been suggested that the philosopher's chief focus was on oppression not exploitation, a fact reinforced by his lack of interest in economic matters. Instead, it is suggested,

> Sartre's political core values can be defined by four primary refusals: no to militarism, no to colonialism, no to discrimination (against women, Jews, blacks, gays), and no to bourgeois morality with its values regarding authority and honor, family and money.
>
> (Betschart, 2019, p. 82)

In this sense, it would seem more plausible to argue that the foundations of contemporary progressivism in contrast to traditional Leftism – an important distinction to which attention needs to be usefully drawn so as to allow us to actively and honestly explore and define a meaningful radical politics (Neiman, 2023) – are perhaps less Foucauldian and more Sartrean. For the purposes of the discussion of existentialism, however, it is of value to remind ourselves that Sartre found it difficult to connect the individualism that he put at the centre of his important philosophy and the political idea that the collective was critical to engendering social change. We find Sartre lapsing into fantastical expectations as he seeks to steer a path through this juxtaposition, expressed in the following crudely mechanistic view of improving the world: 'As soon as there will exist for everyone a margin of real freedom beyond the production of life, Marxism will have lived out its span; a philosophy of freedom will take its place' (Sartre, 1963, p. 34).

I read this as meaning that he sees Marxism as liberatory – a position difficult to cleave to in light of the experience of 'actually existing socialism' since the 1917 Russian Revolution – but envisages the withering away of Marxism if and when freedom is achieved in the same way as Marxism adhered to the view that the dictatorship of the proletariat would lead to the withering away of the state. (History suggests – not surprisingly – that this supposedly scientific dictatorship merely occupied the state structures that people had been assured would simply disappear.) Sartre looks to be suggesting that existentialism – as a philosophy of freedom – would emerge as a dominant force once Marxism had delivered on its ambitions.

This apparently sequential view denies the fact that these two ways of seeing the world and potentially making change therein exist in tension – although it seems reasonable to suggest that a collective means of changing the world needs to be founded on individuals embracing their freedom and making choices to come together to get things done. Indeed, the most powerful and effective action that an individual can take is to mindfully join a collective in order to generate an aggregated power that can serve to make a difference in a social environment. This is a vital act of comradeship which stands in contrast to contemporary notions of allyship, built on unity, a shared perspective, and a commitment to act together to address the systemic limitations rather than leaving those foundations unchallenged.

This takes us back to where we were when we began the exploration of the relationship between the individual and the collective when one considers how one can negotiate the expectations of existentialism when faced with the simple fact that human beings invariably are not found to be living alone but instead share social circumstances alongside myriad others. And all of those in this space are endeavouring to act in good faith by recognising their freedom, their capacity for choice, and the fact that they are responsible for creating meaning and purpose in life in general – and in their lives specifically.

Hence, to conclude this chapter on the existentialist idea of meaning, I will simply note in passing that we need an individual commitment to interpreting the world for ourselves, of course. But equally there will be opportunities to come together in order to generate collective meanings. Sartre's observations about Marxism preceding existentialism seems to pivot around the idea that if you're faced with poverty or find yourself absorbed in the day-to-day work that you are paid to do in an office or a factory, you have no capacity to live your life through freedom and choice (Murphy, 2019).

This disregards the potential of coming together as a group of willing individuals into a collective where you can co-create meanings that may sound loud enough in terms of the numbers involved so as to compete with the dominant meanings that exist. Hence, it is not just about finding meaning in your life but also unearthing and announcing shared meanings amongst those who occupy subaltern roles in our societies.

Ultimately, though, we have a responsibility to create meaning for ourselves in the workplace. But – in light of how we tend to experience organisational life – we have to take into account at the same time that our companies are filled with an abundance of meaning, most of it imposed in that space by those who occupy the senior positions in those hierarchical structures. Moreover, this is all reinforced by the way in which people in this context tend to try to inhabit (or find themselves squeezed into) essentialist roles – and hence experience the denial of the vitality of focusing on one's existence. Our first choice here, then, is to focus on our freedom and choice ... and for our companies to stop filling our work spaces with dominant meanings.

Bibliography

Berson, Y., Oreg, S., & Dvir, T. (2008). CEO values, organizational culture and firm outcomes. *Journal of Organizational Behavior, 5*(29), 615–633.

Betschart, A. (2019). Sartre was not a Marxist. *Sartre Studies International, 25*(2), 77–91.

Brătianu, C., & Bălănescu, G. V. (2008). Vision, mission and corporate values: A comparative analysis of the top 50 US companies. *Management & Marketing, 3*(3), 19–38.

Cole, M., & Higgins, J. (2022). *Leadership Unravelled: The Faulty Thinking behind Modern Management*. Abingdon: Routledge.

Cox, G. (2014). *How to Be an Existentialist – or How to Get Real, Get a Grip and Stop Making Excuses*. London: Bloomsbury.

Davidson, J. D., & Rees-Mogg, W. (1997). *The Sovereign Individual: The Coming Economic Revolution – How to Survive and Prosper in It*. London: Macmillan.

Frankl, V. E. (1946/2004). *Man's Search for Meaning: The Classic Tribute to Hope from the Holocaust*. London: Rider.

Frankl, V. E. (2024). *Embracing Hope: On Freedom, Responsibility and the Meaning of Life*. London: Rider.

Hambrick, D. C., & Mason, P. A. (1984). Upper echelons: The organization as a reflection of its top managers. *Academy of Management Review, 9*(2), 193–206.

Hanaway, M. (2020a). *An Existential Approach to Leadership Challenges*. Abingdon: Routledge.

Hanaway, M. (2020b). *The Handbook of Existential Coaching Practice*. Abingdon: Routledge.

Hiley, D. R. (1987). Power and values in corporate life. *Journal of Business Ethics, 6*(5), 343–353.

Hughes, S. (2025,14 January). UK 'one of the world's least work-oriented countries' says BrewDog founder. Retrieved 17 January 2025, from *The Times*: https://www.thetimes.com/article/85f49fa5-2d41-4799-a076-ece625fcc332?shareToken=49f09e337a0df8d9a330085fd26bd6e9

Hume, D. (1777/1912). *An Enquiry Concerning the Principles of Morals.* Chicago: Open Court Publishing. Retrieved 20 January 2025, from https://davidhume.org/texts/m/9

Jacob, Y. (2019). *An Introduction to Existential Coaching: How Philosophy Can Help Your Clients with Greater Awareness, Courage and Ownership.* Abingdon: Routledge.

Kleiner, A. (2003). *Who Really Matters: The Core Group Theory of Power, Privilege, and Success.* New York: Currency Doubleday.

Link, J. (2004). From the "Power of the Norm" to "Flexible Normalism": Considerations after Foucault. *Cultural Critique, 57*(Spring), 14–32.

Morris, S. (2023, May 25). Bryan Johnson: The tech entrepreneur who spends millions to reverse ageing. Retrieved 21 January 2025, from *The Standard* https://www.standard.co.uk/news/tech/bryan-johnson-tech-millionaire-reverse-ageing-b1083695.html

Murphy, P. A. (2019, 27 December). Did Jean-Paul Sartre fuse existentialism and Marxism? Retrieved 24 January 2025, from *Medium* https://medium.com/@paulaustinmurphy2000/did-jean-paul-sartre-fuse-existentialism-and-marxism-95a127c170e6

Neiman, S. (2023). *Left Is Not Woke.* Cambridge: Polity Press.

O'Connell, M. (2018, February 15). Why Silicon Valley billionaires are prepping for the apocalypse in New Zealand. Retrieved 21 January 2025, from *The Guardian* https://www.theguardian.com/news/2018/feb/15/why-silicon-valley-billionaires-are-prepping-for-the-apocalypse-in-new-zealand

Reed, J. (2025, January 16). Do Indians work too much? Retrieved 16 January 2025, from *Financial Times* FT.com: https://www.ft.com/content/96aefd59-e079-40ae-a334-03c53d02d6a0

Rickles, D. (2022). *Life is Short: An Appropriately Brief Guide to Making It More Meaningful.* Princeton, NJ: Princeton University Press.

Rockwell, D. (2024, February 26). *Do This to Bring Meaning to Work.* Retrieved 20 January 2025, from Leadership Freak: https://leadershipfreak.blog/2024/02/26/do-this-to-bring-meaning-to-work/#:~:text=We%20don't%20find%20meaning,unconditional%20meaningfulness%20in%20rational%20terms.%E2%80%9D

Sample, I. (2022, 17 February). If they could turn back time: How tech billionaires are trying to reverse the ageing process. Retrieved 21 January 2025, from *The Guardian* https://www.theguardian.com/science/2022/feb/17/if-they-could-turn-back-time-how-tech-billionaires-are-trying-to-reverse-the-ageing-process

Sartre, J.-P. (1957/1985). *Existentialism and Human Emotions.* New York: Citadel Press.
Sartre, J.-P. (1963). *Search for a Method.* New York: Alfred A Knopf.
Spivak, G. C. (1988). Can the subaltern speak? In C. Nelson, & L. Grossberg, *Marxism and the Interpretation of Culture* (pp. 271–313). Basingstoke: Macmillan.
Suarez-Battan, M. (2021, 16 December). *The Rise of the Imagination Worker.* Retrieved 20 January 2025, from Forbes https://www.forbes.com/sites/mural/2021/12/13/the-rise-of-the-imagination-worker/#:~:text=Henry%20Ford%20even%20once%20lamented,by%20robots%20%E2%80%94%20if%20they%20existed.
Thomas-Olalde, O., & Velho, A. (2011). Othering and its effects – exploring the concept. In H. Niedrig, & C. Ydesen, *Writing Postcolonial Histories of Intercultural Education* (pp. 27–51). Frankfurt: Peter Lang.

The burden of choice 5

I am the sum of my choices

Back in March 2023, three years after Covid had launched itself around the world and led me to isolate myself completely, my wife made a plan for the family to fly out to Spain to visit her brother and sister-in-law, who had recently relocated there. Mindful of my continuing and debilitating anxiety, Sarah broached the topic with me, indicating that she assumed that I would not be able to come, given the state of my mental health. It took a mere moment for me to respond that I would struggle to make such a trip … yet minutes after this exchange, as I sat quietly at my desk mulling it all over, I was consumed by another anxiety altogether, namely that my family would be travelling without me … and that I desperately needed to be with them.

Eventually, it was agreed that flights would be booked for all of us, although there was a possibility that I might not be able to travel. However, I was completely committed to finding a way to make the trip … and spent quite a lot of time in my psychotherapy sessions talking about how I felt about it all and how best I might 'loosen the grip' of Covid (a term that my excellent therapist Malcolm offered as a way of conceptualising how best to manage my anxiety) and find a means by which to make the journey. We focused, for example, on what would be positive about going out to Andalusia: first and foremost, I wanted to be in the sun with my son on the beach, but the other incentive was the idea of being in a delightful Spanish square, drinking a cool *cerveza* or sherry and eating a bowl of olives or almonds!

On the morning of the flight, it was a 4.50am alarm call and, as soon as I surfaced, I was conscious of feeling pressured and panicked, with a blood

DOI: 10.4324/9781003592624-5

pressure reading that was extremely high. I drove us all to Stansted airport and was immediately taken by how familiar and unchanged everything appeared: it looked no different to the time when I had last flown from there before the pandemic, so it left me confronted with the curious idea that actually the world at large looked as though nothing had happened. I drew up in the car park more or less in front of the terminal, where I had parked on many occasions, and wandered through the labyrinth of ramps, steps and lifts to get into Departures.

I was mindful of people around me – closer to me than people had been other than my family for three or so years. My anxiety symptoms were thrumming away in the background, but it felt as though I could hold them there and not allow them to burst forth and derail me. The Departure area was thronged with an extraordinary number of people, something that caused me to catch my breath and lose a little control. As we approached Security, I was faced with snaking queues, people pressed up against one another, as if getting closer to the person ahead of you would somehow make the line go quicker. Beyond that, I could see large numbers of people milling around – and I was able then to envisage the gates and the planes.

As a mental image, the idea of the planes was particularly disruptive in terms of my emotions: I recalled previous economy flights, crushed into close proximity with others … and the way in which so many passengers leap from their seat upon landing as soon as the seatbelt sign goes off, and cause an overbearing sense of congestion (and, for me, claustrophobia) as soon as they are up on their feet, filling the aisle and thrusting their sweaty backsides in the faces of passengers who choose not to join this crazed melee. Standing on that threshold, it felt as though my options had evaporated and that circumstances were now dictating that I would not be able to board the plane.

Tearfully, I stood stock still, staring into what looked to me to be a hyperactive morass of people, loading their bags, coats and shoes into trays and onto conveyors and walking through metal detectors. I found myself saying, "I can't do this", aware that I could not allow my situation to prevent the family from making the trip, so seeking to play it down as best I could. Eventually, the two of them hugged and reassured me, before making their way into what looked to me to be an unruly crush of bodies. I proceeded to stand there alone for a further 20 minutes, my gaze fixed on the people penned between the snaking belt barriers. I hoped I could eventually find the capacity to walk through and join them.

In the end, the bustle around me as I stood in the middle of Departures and that sight of a mass of people with no sign of social distancing compelled me to reluctantly turn my back and amble disconsolately to the

Arrivals area of the airport. After pausing for some food and a coffee, I made my way in despair to the car, aware now that I would not now be with them for this trip and hence already missing them.

I tried to hide behind my diagnosis, ascribing my inability to fly to the condition I had developed in light of the circumstances I had faced in Spring 2020. But in reality I was aware even then – and so much more so now – that not boarding that flight was a choice that I made. As my psychotherapist regularly reminds me, anxiety is best thought of not as a pathology but as a feature of the human condition, a mental and bodily reaction to the fact that life is full of risk and we each of us have to assess it in the moment. Clearly, there are occasions where we find ourselves oppressively amplifying it – but broadly it is a prompt to compel us in our existence to consider the risk we face and shape our response to that accordingly.

It was not an act of bad faith on my part not to board the plane. However, my efforts to blame my experience of anxiety throughout that time – and, to an extent, up to the present day – for my failure to fly that day obscures the fact that it was – at the end of the day – my choice. This, of course, is difficult for me to admit, as a person who considers themself to have agency in the world. I did not want to be personally responsible for not travelling with my family … but that responsibility did indeed lie solely with me. Ultimately, when confronting the either/or that morning, I could have flown or not flown but, in the end, I actively chose the latter option, based on a calculation that encompassed a number of variables, such as: What if I had an episode once I'd boarded that delayed the plane or forced it to land? How would I cope with being in such close contact with people when I had isolated myself hugely over the previous three years? Could I cope with being that far away from what I saw more and more as the safety of home?

I chose not to go. I appraised the situation and made a decision on the basis of what I thought and how I felt. No one – and nothing else – can be held to account for that choice. It was easy to tell people that the anxiety stopped me from travelling but it was my reaction to that circumstance and my consideration of the options that led me – as an existing human being – to decide to step back and away from the chance to spend a few days in Spain.

I am still embarrassed by this episode – but pleased that, just a year or so later, I made a different decision when faced with another jaunt to Spain. I was able to board the plane and even found myself sitting in the familiar cramped conditions of a budget airline flight thinking how it felt entirely natural for me to be there. In a Freudian sense, my first effort to fly after the pandemic was an uncanny experience: everything looked familiar yet – beneath the surface – I sensed that things were very different (Freud, 2003). By the second attempt, the uncanniness had eased so far into the background that it was manageable.

Choosing not to choose is a choice

All of which is a reminder that we can so often delude ourselves into thinking that a course of action that we have taken was foisted upon us by circumstances, meaning that it cannot be seen to be a choice on our part. But, as suggested above, many of even the most complicated – or, indeed, complex – decisions are processed by us at a relatively superficial level as a "go/no go" construct. This crude binary often appears in corporate life, as managers look to consider whether to sanction a project or pull the plug on it. These discussions are often surrounded by volumes of what is deemed to be relevant data – and decisions are said to be made in light of a rationale that arises out of a metricised view of the world.

In such circumstances, people can be seen to be hiding behind the idea that the world can be conveniently quantified and rationalised. It can sometimes be the case that people throw up their hands and declare that they had no choice but to do whatever it was that they ended up doing, in light of the information surrounding the decision that they were facing. Yet the choice is made. I recently hosted a conversational event around the topic of how people in the workplace might be finding ways to resist in a context where our managers are now described as "leaders" – and, by implication, the rest of us need to be thought of as "followers". The discussion took us to a place where we acknowledged that every human agent – notwithstanding where they sit in a hierarchy – is doubtless wrestling with anxieties which, to an extent, are contained by the organisational context, until such time as that framework wobbles for whatever reason (Lyth, 1988).

As we spoke about this, someone referred to the fact that the ever-expanding volume of data that senior people in organisations tend to demand ahead of a decision is akin to a security blanket, such as the one that Linus van Pelt constantly has in his arms in the *Peanuts* cartoons. This is invariably seen as a protection from the anguish of coming to terms with being alive in the world. From a psychoanalytic perspective, though, Linus's blanket – and other similar items in the life of a child – are deemed to serve a purpose in allowing development from one state to another, a journey towards psychological independence. It is argued that:

> It is not the object, of course, that is transitional. The object represents the infant's transition from a state of being merged with the mother to a state of being in relation to the mother as something outside and separate.
>
> (Winnicott, 1989, pp. 14–15)

For Linus, it would seem, he has failed to make that transition and is stuck with a reliance on the object. And we can perhaps see something similar taking place in far too many boardrooms, where the anxiety of having to make a choice is delayed or assuaged by an ever-expanding volume of data.

Trying to convince yourself of things you don't believe in your heart

The last time I rewatched the film *Casablanca* (1942) I was very much taken by Rick Blaine's existentialism in terms of how the lead character lives his life and the choices that he has made – and that he goes on to make in light of the circumstances with which he is confronted in the movie. A broken heart compelled him to abandon his previous self, which was positively engaged with the world. He disappeared to Casablanca. When asked why he chose to go there, he jokingly replies that it was because of the water. He is promptly reminded that he is in the desert! He has patently chosen to absent himself from his previous life ... but seems, at points in the story, to be indicating that this was foisted upon him by being ignominiously dumped by his lover, Ilsa, in Paris on the day that the Germans marched into the city. It is doubtful that the character would acknowledge this, but he chooses to swim around in a whisky glass, drowning his sorrows.

At one point, Victor Laszlo, the man who turns out to be Ilsa's husband and who she assumed had died in a German concentration camp due to his vocal and active opposition to the Nazi regime and so did not feel that her affair with Rick was an infidelity, is having a challenging conversation with Rick. In an interesting analysis of this exchange, it is suggested that this discussion can be seen to occur with Rick Blaine in *Casablanca*, but could equally be happening with the character of Roquentin in Sartre's novel *Nausea* – or, indeed, with Sartre himself. In essence, Laszlo inquires as to whether Rick is aware of the fact that he is looking to escape from himself, an activity in which he will never find success (Kellman, 1983, p. 112).

We are our existence, which entails – on a moment-by-moment basis – having to accept the freedom that we experience in life and be aware of the fact that we face myriad choices. To attempt to deny this, as Laszlo suggests, is to engage in something that we can never achieve, namely separating ourselves from how we live. That is not to say that we are not constantly confronted by circumstances that place boundaries around the choices that we are making. But our authentic self from an existentialist perspective openly acknowledges that – and consequently makes choices in the knowledge of the restraints that partly inhibit the range of those choices.

This complexity in respect to choice is important in terms of how we actively opt to live our life moment to moment. And, in the workplace, that is made all the more difficult, as, in a liberal democratic context, we are ideologically envisaged as human agents who are capable of participating actively in society. Notwithstanding the grandiose corporate statements about speaking up and staff engagement, my experience has been that organisational life is tightly constrained – and my liberty as a human being is more tightly managed, directly and through cultural expectations – than is the case in wider society. That said, the appearance of freedom of choice is often challenged by our experience when we are immersed in the actuality of our existence in a range of contexts.

For example, in a capitalist society, it is ideologically asserted that we are confronted with multiple opportunities for choice, especially as a consumer. In the Cold War, the self-declared "free world" was argued to stand in contrast to the Communist bloc; specifically, the distinction was constantly made between the abundance of a range of products on shop shelves in the former and the paucity of choice in the latter. A US sociologist in the post-war period offered a fictional analysis of his country's attempt to undermine the Stalinist states by bombarding them not with missiles but instead with consumer goods, under the operational name of *Operation Abundance* – and the popular label of *The Nylon War*. Undergirding this was the following theory: '[I]f allowed to sample the riches of America, the Russian people would not long tolerate masters who gave them tanks and spies instead of vacuum cleaners and beauty parlours' (Riesman, 1951, p. 163).

Consumer choice?

Riesman's analysis was a means by which to raise the way in which capitalism juxtaposed itself with communism at a subtle ideological level. A land of plenty in contrast to a land of poverty. Undergirding this notion, of course, is the simple assumption that consumers in the West were offered extensive choices that they were free to make. I recall the first time that I ever visited a supermarket in the US back in the 1990s, I was flabbergasted by the number of brands of bland orange cheese that could be found on the shelves. They all looked the same, apart from the label on the packaging, and no doubt all pretty much tasted the same … yet it certainly offered an illusion of choice to the shoppers as they trundled around these cathedrals of abundance.

In a piece of existential-phenomenological research that explores the experience of people facing this type of choice, three important themes that impacted the idea that people enjoyed absolute liberty were identified. These stand separate to the more obvious issue of whether a person has the money required to buy what they need or what they would like: Waitrose and M&S may offer a rich variety of exciting foods to buy but the ability to access those goods in a capitalist society depends on how much money you have and – more subtly – how comfortable you feel about fitting into these specific socio-economic contexts. As for the three significantly more subtle factors that are argued to frame our consumer choices, the first is said to be whether we feel restricted or free from restrictions. Interestingly, people in the research suggested that they felt more restricted when faced with decisions for which they were completely responsible. Unsurprisingly, there was distance for these shoppers – all women in quite traditionally gendered roles at that time – between 'have to have' items and "nice to have" products (Thompson et al., 1990, p. 353).

The second element was seen to be the extent to which people felt in control or out of control, with the latter manifesting itself most apparently when the shopper "falls in love" with something and buys it on impulse. It is suggested that this raises an issue of the way in which our choice might be impacted by the extent to which we are seeking to be practical and the very human emotion of feeling excited about something (Thompson et al. 1990, p. 354). The final question was said to be the extent to which the people were being captivated or being deliberate: the former is deemed to be an emotional and relatively unthinking immersion in the act of shopping, whilst the latter speaks to a more rationalised and evaluative approach to consuming (Thompson et al. 1990, p. 356).

This led the authors to conclude that avoiding restrictions, having a sense of control, and luxuriating in the sensuality of consuming were optimal in terms of experiencing choice in this context. However, they also identified some interesting tensions in this regard, namely that '

> participants sometimes experienced more freedom when placed in a restricted situation and gained a feeling of control by giving up

> control, and some felt the reasoned course of action was to be more impulsive (and less rationalistic) in their shopping decisions.
>
> (Thompson et al. 1990, p. 358)

All of which serves as an important reminder that our experiences as human agents embracing choice are very likely to be far from straightforward. While the findings arose from people's experiences of shopping, there is no doubt that our experience of choice in the workplace is likely to be similarly overwritten by a range of issues. And, while the notion of expansive choice in a consumer context might quite reasonably be seen to dominate the discourse that exists in our contemporary society, there feels to be slightly more liberty at play in this context than one might find in organisational life. In the supermarket, I may get to choose from a wide range of brands of a similar product – tinned soup, for example – but at work it feels predominantly as though most of my choices are being made for me, made by the leader(s) that I am expected to follow.

Controlling my choices

When considering how human beings are required to constantly make decisions, reference is made to the "pathos of action", where it is recognised that running through the sequence of choices that someone makes across the course of their life achieves both self-fulfilment and self-renunciation. Hence, it is argued that:

> Decision brings the existent face to face with himself in a way that must stir anxiety. Thus most of us hate to make decisions of any magnitude. We avoid them or postpone them for as long as we can. For if to decide is on the one hand to thrust forward into a new level of existence, it is on the other hand to take the risk of cutting oneself off from the other possibilities that were open. It is to pledge or engage one's future, and since no one can foresee the future, such an engagement is always freighted with risk and attended by anxiety.
>
> (Macquarrie, 1973, pp. 182–183)

We are all to an extent aware of the fact that there is no choice without sacrifice. These days, this recognition arises in the language of psychobabble as an "opportunity cost", a notion that sounds as if it owes more to economics than it does to existing in the world. If we return to the aerodrome at the end of *Casablanca*, we find Rick trying to persuade Ilsa to leave with her husband, despite the obvious rekindling of their affair that began in Paris. He memorably advises her that, 'If that plane leaves the ground and you're not with him, you'll regret it. Maybe not today. Maybe not tomorrow, but soon and for the rest of your life.' (IMDb, n.d.). This is the most powerful statement, perhaps, of the impact of choice on us, although this exchange seems to depart from existentialism insofar as Rick is defining what and how Ilsa will feel … and only Ilsa herself, engaging with the world and making decisions therein, is in a position to experience the impact of the sacrifice that occurs in light of having made a choice.

This is underscored by the observation that 'it is in action, including thought, freedom, and decision, that man is most truly and fully himself' (Macquarrie, 1973, p. 188) And Sartre provides insight into how we are all compelled to navigate choice when he argues:

> In one sense choice is possible, but what is not possible is not to choose. I can always choose, but I must know that if I do not choose, that is still a choice. This, although it may appear merely formal, is of great importance as a limit to fantasy and caprice. For, when I confront a real situation – for example, that I am a sexual being, able to have relations with a being of the other sex and able to have children – I am obliged to choose my attitude to it, and in every respect I bear the responsibility of the choice which, in committing myself, also commits the whole of humanity.
>
> (Sartre, 1948/1973, p. 48)

We are not merely creatures in a Skinnerite maze, following a path to one outcome or another. We are choosing our actions in the world – but, prior to that, we are making a choice as to what we think about the circumstances that surround the decision that confronts us. For example, when I was presented with the opportunity to take voluntary redundancy, I pondered the practicalities of this, in terms of whether I would find work as a freelance and the extent to which I could survive financially in such a changed circumstance. But there was also due consideration of what it would mean for me and how it might feel to no longer be in structured work. Similarly, I felt forced to confront the fact that I no longer felt ethically able to remain in an organisation which I was no longer convinced was contributing positively to the overall domain in which it functioned. These choices had to be made in advance of the practical "go/no go" choice in regard to the settlement.

Choosing choice

The double-stranded quality of human choice is important when we come to consider how we make our choices in life – and the freedom and constraints that exist in that respect. In Figure 5.1, the act of choice in the world is foregrounded; in this instance, we are confronted with three options, marked as A, B, and C. But life is not a multiple-choice exam. The practicalities of deciding which of these we should opt for is not merely a matter of picking one from three, simply by comparing one to another. When I was considering voluntary redundancy, it would have been easy to declare that there were simply two options from which to choose: take the money and run; or sit tight and suck it up. But active in the background were multiple choices of thought and attitude that – as a human agent – I needed to make before I could begin to think about the apparent either/or with which I was confronted.

Seeing one's being

As part of our day-to-day existence, we need to be attentive to the circumstances in which we find ourselves, many of which are of our own

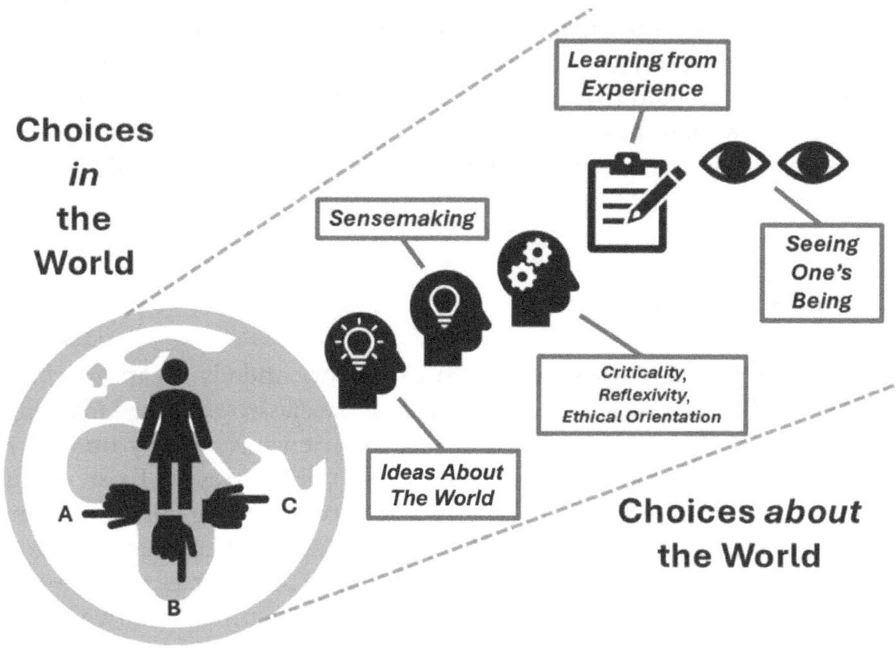

FIGURE 5.1 Thinking about choices in life

making and others are imposed on us by others – for example, in considering the workplace, this might mean a manager looking to impose their will on us or indeed a group of people with whom we work affecting us in light of their collective will. In the latter instance, this effect might be obtained simply by those people coming together to speak with a unified voice (even when that collective position might actually be sustained regardless of the fact that some disagree with it but assume a coherence of everybody and so choose silence themselves). This, of course, is referred to as pluralistic ignorance, which suggests that:

> we are likely to consistently misinterpret the strength of dominant positions and thence to assume our perspective to be subaltern, peripheral, and the opinion of a minority … This complicity with a consensus that does not exist serves to render us silent at precisely the time when our voices are perhaps most needed.
>
> (Cole & Higgins, 2023, pp. 66–67)

This is where we begin in Figure 5.1, with a focus on our immersion in experience and the need to pay attention to what we are seeing all around us in the world where we need to embrace our freedom and make our choices. This attention also works at two levels: firstly, we are looking outside of our selves at what surrounds us – including the population of which we are a part; and, secondly, we need to be mindful of what is occurring for us internally, in regard to our reactions, our feelings, our thoughts, and our ideas. This is what is meant in the diagram by the phrase "seeing our being": we are recognising our existence in the world – and the way in which we are experiencing that environment.

Learning from experience

People often speak of learning from experience merely as an approach that can be thought of as standing in contrast to classroom-based teaching. Pedagogically, this is taken to mean that experience is actively utilised as material upon which one might reflect and derive insight. Existentially, though, there is no separation whatsoever between being and developing an understanding of that being. If we are mindful of all that is around us – and within us – and see that being in rich terms, it is also the case that we are living our life and learning at the same time. The two things are seamless, because to separate the two conceptually is to create an artificial barrier between experience and understanding. Instead, despite the fact that two different labels are being applied to aspects of human experience, it is the case that this distinction is completely artificial and needs to be erased.

Criticality, reflexivity, ethics

The learning we derive from simultaneously experiencing and understanding life is not a final destination in terms of thoughtfully engaging with the challenges of existence. We need to subject this active awareness to careful consideration through three key prisms, namely *criticality*, *reflexivity*, and *ethics* (Cole & Higgins, 2023, pp. 218–219). In the first instance, we need to engage with life *critically*, seeking to question everything. This is not about merely being a contrarian but instead it sees us looking at ourselves and everything that surrounds our existence in a way that challenges the taken-for-granted and common sense. For instance, there is an urgent need for us to find our voices and *ask the questions* that occur to us in light of the life that we are living and that we see around us. But, at the same time, we need to embrace an even deeper criticality informed by the thinking that underpins existentialism by reminding ourselves then to *question the answers*. This is what deep criticality looks like.

Secondly, we need to abandon the notion of reflecting on the world and activity therein as if it is something from which we can abstract ourselves. Too much reflective practice seems founded on the notion that we can generate a distance in order to explore circumstances in the world. In reality, of course, we are an intrinsic part of that world and our presence and action therein shapes it intimately. To underscore this point, if we find ourselves standing in a forest, we cannot escape the fact that we are an integral part of that woodland. This extends right down to the fact that there is a tiny part of the forest that I cannot see because I am standing on it. I cannot reflect upon the forest as if it were external to me because being there means that I am actively shaping it. This, then, is what is meant when we speak of *reflexivity*: I am considering how it is to be me in the forest – and how my being there alters it.

Lastly, it is vital that we explore our learning in a way that encourages us to develop our ethical selves. Rationalism and scientism, in league with an ongoing fascination with quantification and its measurability, tend to draw us away from the practicality of what it means to be alive in the world. Our autoethnographic perspectives tend to get subsumed by a social trend towards collapsing human experience and the world at large into bundles of numbers or graphic representations of them, such as tables and graphs.

This tendency is particularly noticeable in corporate contexts, especially the managerial aspects of the workplace. Regrettably, this focus can too often lead to an effacement of our fundamental human need to think ethically about our presence in the world, which is particularly important from the position of an atheistic existentialism.

The major religions provide a background to morality; this can sometimes be boiled down to the simple equation that you should aim to do good in the world so as to avoid a god's punishment. But it is suggested that, from a Sartrean perspective, 'values cannot be anything but the result of the initial choice made by each human being; in other words, they can never be "recognized" or "discovered"' (Marcel, 1946/2018, p. 96). This means that ethics do not derive from an external yet coherent view of the world but instead emerge in the course of each individual's choices. We have moved from morality arising out of the Ten Commandments to an ethics defined by thousands upon thousands of actions in the world.

This can lead some to conclude that existentialism cannot be relied upon to be ethical in practice due to two reasons. Firstly, it is a view of the world that is wholly ontological. This is seen to mean in practice that existentialism looks to *describe* the world as it is rather than explore how the world *ought* to be. And the second reason that people contest its ability to offer an ethical orientation is that it appears to encourage a moral subjectivism, wherein 'morality is simply a matter of individual preferences' (Crowe, 2024, p. 91). But it is possible to take the view that actually the freedom enjoyed by each individual requires them to navigate the world by making choices but also demands that they exercise that same freedom in order to be ethical.

It is certainly the case that even those steeped in religious belief still have to actively subscribe to moral precepts such as the Golden Rule, which states that we should do unto others as we would have them do unto us (Singer, 1963). This despite the fact that this notion appears across the widest range of religions throughout history: the principle can be found expressed in various ways in all three of the Abrahamic religions, as well as *inter alia* in Hinduism and Taoism. But – as Kierkegaard's work firmly establishes – the individual has to actively choose to embrace this precept as a defining way of being in the world; just being steeped in the faith and its associated tradition does not necessarily mean that a person is actively living their life in a way that embraces this view of the world and our relations therein.

Reminding ourselves to engage with the world in a way that mindfully interrogates the status quo locates us firmly in the midst of life instead of viewing life almost as something external to us, and putting ethical considerations at the heart of our thinking and actions in the world is existentially essential, as we have seen. It also leads us into a space where we can apply ourselves to try and make sense of our lives and the lives of others alongside whom we find ourselves thrown. I am using the term sensemaking here purposefully, as there is a danger in a society dominated by an overbearing rationalism that we seek instead to engage in *interpretation*, something far too often seen in the workplace context in terms of relations between people.

Sensemaking

The problem with this is that it is a perspective that effectively puts us at a conceptual distance to the world, even though that is a place in which we find ourselves and which is both complicated and complex. It presupposes a decisive and definitive knowability of the space and time in which we find ourselves. In that sense, it seeks to diminish the absurdity that can be seen to be integral to our existence. Instead, to focus on sensemaking – an approach to the world very successfully articulated by Brenda Dervin – it is important to acknowledge that the sensemaking methodology is 'grounded philosophically and theoretically within a phenomenological and interpretive perspective which makes explicit ontological and epistemological assumptions' (Naumer et al., 2008, p. 506).

In terms of describing this approach, a metaphor is offered in terms of a graphic representation of a person making their way in life, surrounded by the wide range of contextual issues that they face in that moment and finding a way in which to bridge a gap in their existential understanding. In describing this representation, it is observed that:

> a person is seen as embedded in a context-laden situation, bounded in time-space. The person pictured as crossing a bridge is used to metaphorically describe the way that humans are mandated by the human condition to bridge gaps in an always evolving and ever-gappy "reality." The person is seen facing a gap (i.e., a sense-making need) that arises out of a situation. Through the process of gap bridging, people seek inputs (sometimes the stuff systems call information) and engage in other activities through the time-space continuum that lead to outcomes.
>
> (Naumer et al., 2008, p. 506)

Dervin's vision of sensemaking resonates helpfully with existentialism given the shared interest of the two approaches in phenomenology, an immersion in – and acute awareness of – the facts of simply being a human agent in the world. Usefully, it is also the case that it allows for a collective appreciation of circumstances that we face – or the "gaps", as Dervin's approach indicates. To understand the practice of this approach, another definition of the work of sensemaking is useful at this point:

> By sensemaking, modern researchers seem to mean something different from creativity, comprehension, curiosity, mental modeling, explanation, or situational awareness, although all these factors or phenomena can be involved in or related to sensemaking. Sensemaking is a motivated, continuous effort to understand connections (which can be among people, places, and events) in order to anticipate their trajectories and act effectively.
>
> (Klein et al., 2006, p. 71)

Ideas about the world

Paying attention to our being, whilst – at the same time – looking to learn from that experience, interrogate it in a number of ways, and make sense of it (as opposed to scientifically interpreting it and offering some quantitative assessment of it), leads us to generate not merely an appreciation of the world in which we find ourselves but some meaningful ideas about what we have experienced and how we might choose to live our lives.

These are the ideas about the world that emerge from our effort to deeply immerse ourselves in all facets of our existence in order to: be conscious of the dynamics that surround us; create a provisional sense of understanding of where we are and what we are facing as opposed to a fixed and scientific interpretation of that context; and use this insight so as to consider our freedom and the choices we are able to make, while – at the same time – using this way of being in the world based upon an alertness on a moment-by-moment basis in order to develop our own personal moral compass.

Returning to Figure 5.1, we are reminded that – in practical terms – we constantly face the anguish of having to make choices as an integral and continuous part of our day-to-day lives, as opposed to the act of choosing being seen as a sequence of separate events that punctuate our existence. But the way in which we can effectively navigate the fact that choice is an implicit part of our very existence is to be aware that, in the background and on a constant basis, we are engaging with the world into which we have been thrown. This entails pulling the business of being to the forefront of our existence, in order that we can then scrutinise it and draw out key thoughts and ideas from that in order to understand what we have done … and think carefully about what we are minded to do next.

The choice of choice

As I cast a glance around all the various facets of my life, I can very often feel utterly constrained. Across my 40 years in the workplace as part of a workforce, it very often felt as though I was a mere reed in the wind, bending and adapting to the gusts of opinion and instruction that buffeted me from every direction. Most of the time, I did what I was told, particularly if the direction to do something came from those above me. Similarly, my need to be part of the gang, when – for most of my life – I had been outside the gang and an object of their derision and hostility, meant that I tended to comply with the collective view even on those occasions when in my heart I disagreed with it. A powerful reminder of how ostracism is so very difficult for human beings to endure.

It seems pretty certain that my perspective now, in terms of a fascination with voice, silence, and power in the workplace, derives in part from the fact that I spent so much time keeping schtum, keeping my head down, and getting stuff done in the way in which it had been suggested that I do it. In that sense, over recent years, I have chosen to revisit my experiences and embrace a different way of being over the course of the past nine years. It was a change of environment – a shift from the command-and-control and performance-obsessed world of frontline NHS organisations to the spaciousness and liberation of a role in the NHS London Leadership Academy – which created the circumstances for me to make that change.

But it is important to focus on the fact that – notwithstanding where we find ourselves in terms of our existence – we are always making a choice, even if, as in my case, it was to choose not to rock the boat and simply follow orders in the workplace. It is not just a question of stepping into the agency of choice and making some grand gesture or adjustment in how one lives one's life: it is also very much about openly acknowledging to oneself that simply navigating the day-to-day sees me making multiple choices … and I need to be aware when those choices are not necessarily to opt to do what I would most like to do in any given circumstance.

In terms of existentialism, both Kierkegaard and Sartre offer us an insight into the complexity of living a life that is full of choice, whether we like it or not. The latter, of course, notably took the view that we are the sum of our choices, insofar as existence precedes essence. By way of defining this central precept, he argues 'Man is nothing else but what he makes of himself' (Sartre, 1957/1985, p. 15). Crucially, the individual is seen to emerge from nothingness – so, it is only through their presence in the world that they define themselves. This is why the concept of freedom and choice is so essential to the Sartrean perspective.

This position is based upon an interesting perspective, namely that freedom is a constant – even for those whose liberty has been removed. It is argued that

> Sartre maintains that if a being is free, he is always free, in all situations, under all circumstances. In classical theories of freedom we are said to be free at certain moments and not free at certain others. But Sartre tells us that if man is free, he is always free. It would be incomprehensible, he argues, that freedom should disappear and then reappear at some later moment.
>
> (Wahl, 1959/2019, p. 60)

However, as we have previously seen, Sartre's notion of facticity reminds us that, whilst we are thrown into the world and have to immediately start to make our way in it, we land in a context that restricts us in some ways – but also reminds us of the freedom we have to wriggle free of those constraints, or to accept circumstances that we cannot at that moment change.

In respect to Kierkegaard's efforts to interrogate the relationship between human existence and Christian faith, the philosopher is powerfully drawn to the linked issues of freedom, choice, and responsibility. His work of 1843 underscores that, in that it challenges the reader with two perspectives on life and goes under the title *Either/Or*. In an introduction to this work, the following observation about the quality and character of the text is offered:

> [O]ne cannot immediately assume that the point or significance of Either/Or is adequately put by saying that the work provides readers with the opportunity to ask themselves which of the two points of view represented they themselves prefer. Many questions intervene. Just how distinct are the two points of view? Why can't they be combined? What if we don't feel like assenting to either? And isn't it really obvious that we are supposed to assent in the end to the ethical point of view anyway? But then what if I don't feel like doing that? Must I conclude that I've missed something, or is it because something is missing in me?
>
> (Hannay, 1843/1992, pp. 4–5)

This reminds us how choice in the world has to run alongside choice in respect to our perspective on the world. Kierkegaard's work appears to present us literally with two positions – the aesthetic and the ethical – but we cannot possibly make a judgement between these apparent alternatives without engaging with the world in a way that takes us below the superficial helter-skelter of day-to-day existence and requires us to engage intellectually with it.

We have already touched upon how Sartre considers people might engage ethically with their freedom and their capacity to make choices. Kierkegaard, it is suggested, offers a view which states that our freedom allows us to choose to do wrong. A person, for example, might opt to live exclusively for themselves. But this is taken to mean that 'if such a life-choice is to be genuine, then commitment to it must be made explicit – it must be recognised as consciously chosen rather than externally compelled – and once this occurs, the choice of wrongdoing leads inevitably to guilt and, ultimately for Kierkegaard, to repentance' (Michelman, 2010, p. 92).

The communal context of choice

Given the time we spend in the workplace, we need to ensure that we are mindful of the freedom that we have and the capacity for choice. We have noted that there are limitations placed on that – but to accept those limitations is to make a choice to do precisely that. Existentialism offers no way of avoiding the act of choosing – and denies us the opportunity to hide behind circumstances or the actions of others in order to justify what we ultimately opt to do. The phrases "I had no choice" and "I had to do that" simply are not part of the vernacular of this approach to human life. Thinking that we're not making a choice is a major choice in itself.

Alongside confronting this powerful fact, there is a linked but separate consideration in regard to the contexts in which we consider the two levels of choice, these being the way in which we choose how we understand our life in the world, which in turn actively informs the practical choices with which we find ourselves confronted constantly in our lives, including in our lives in the workplace. Existentialism is often seen as an overbearingly individualistic take on the world, one where the human subject holds all of the responsibility for their existence and makes their choices in complete isolation.

In a conversation I was having with a colleague this morning, we were discussing corporate life and the way in which we are very often present in this environment. Organisational structures tend to paradoxically fetishise two things: the sovereign individual and also the artificial and imposed notion of the team. The former is viewed as entirely separate from the extensive terrain in which they sit, although the term "team" is imported into our business structures in order to tame those individuals. They are kept separate from others by putting them in close proximity – and explicit arrangements for oversight – to an agreed group of people around them.

Ultimately, though, our existence occurs alongside and in conjunction with others. We sit in the midst of an ever-shifting and remarkably flexible mesh, made up of everyone around us, as far as we can see. We make choices, of course, in terms of how intimate or distanced we choose to be from this wider panorama ... and contemporary workplace politics has actively sought to diminish the allure of attending to that connectivity, as the workplace has seen a tendency to move away from the support that can derive from collectivity. But ultimately we exercise our freedom and make our choices in a connected space, somewhere in which we need to be mindful of how our decisions are experienced by both ourselves and others ... and also how we may choose at certain points to subsume ourselves as part of a group for a given period and link together with others in order to make collective decisions, potentially preceding collective actions.

This is also an important reminder to those who manage the workplace that freedom is an implicit element of human existence ... and to attempt to deny that to those around you is an active refusal of a fundamental quality of their existence. Far too often, those in charge interpret their status as meaning that they have to have absolute control of what is going on around them – and of the people that the organisation positions them above or alongside. In so doing, they can be seen to be adversely affecting the freedom of other human agents – and they are accorded this entitlement simply on the basis of where they have landed in a hierarchical organisational structure.

This should give us pause for a moment to wonder aloud whether the contemporary and conjoined notions of leadership and followership actually artificially fly in the face of a fundamental right for a living person to exercise as much freedom and choice as possible, particularly in the workplace. Those who occupy the role of leader can be seen to be actively inhibiting the freedom that every person sharing this relatively tiny planet, spinning around in the void, should feel to be their entitlement, not solely in terms of an employment contract, a legal framework, or even a human right, but instead as an undeniable element of simply finding oneself thrown into existence and then confronting the finitude associated with that tenure.

While we may also actively choose followership, the question then arises as to whether we make that choice in light of the constraints that exist in terms of the facticity of human life. This, of course, is often varnished with a sense of corporate arrangements as currently constituted being in some way almost God-given, and hence unquestionable and unchallengeable. Often, we opt for silence in the face of the notion of followership, simply because the apparent permanence of the structure denies us the opportunity to think critically about it and then to voice aloud our reservations about the status quo and how it might be denying us as human beings in the midst of being in the world.

There is no easy answer here, because existence is a challenging place to find oneself. But a starting point for everyone pivots around freedom, choice, and responsibility – and demands that we ask ourselves one or two questions, depending on where we find ourselves in the world of work:

> How have I ended up being described as a leader in the current context … and how am I experienced in that role by everyone in the wider social mesh with whom I am connected?
>
> As someone described as a leader, to what extent do my thoughts, ideas, and choices adversely impact the basic existential freedom of those around me?
>
> How content am I with being thought of as a follower – and what does it mean to me to occupy that role, in terms of how I experience being with others in and around my workplace?
>
> How can I best work to support the freedom of others, while – at the same time – ensuring my own freedom to make the choices I need to make in order to live my temporally limited life as much to the full as possible?

Bibliography

Cole, M., & Higgins, J. (2023). *The Great Unheard at Work: Understanding Voice and Silence in Organisations*. Abingdon: Routledge.

Crowe, J. (2024, 1 August). Is an existentialist ethics possible? *The Ultimate Guide – Existentialism. Philosophy Now, 90–92*.

Freud, S. (2003). *The Uncanny (Penguin Modern Classics)*. London: Penguin.

Hannay, A. (1843/1992). Introduction. In S. Kierkegaard, *Either/Or: A Fragment of Life* (pp. 1–21). London: Penguin.

IMDb. (n.d.). *Casablanca Quotes*. Retrieved 11 February 2025, from IMDb: https://www.imdb.com/title/tt0034583/quotes

Kellman, S. G. (1983). Everybody comes to Roquentin's: "La Nausée" and "Casablanca". *Mosaic, 16*(1/2), 103–112.

Klein, G., Moon, B., & Hoffman, R. R. (2006, July/August). Making sense of sensemaking 1: Alternative perspectives. *IEEE Intelligent Systems, 21*(4), 70–73.

Lewin, K., Lippitt, R., & White, R. K. (1939). Patterns of aggressive behavior in experimentally created social climates. *Journal of Social Psychology*, 10, 271–301.
Lyth, I. M. (1988). *Containing Anxiety in Institutions: Selected Essays Volume One.* London: Free Association Books.
Macquarrie, J. (1973). *Existentialism.* Harmondsworth: Penguin.
Marcel, G. (1946/2018). *The Philosophy of Existence.* Providence, RI: Cluny Media.
Michelman, S. (2010). *The A to Z of Existentialism.* Lanham, MD: The Scarecrow Press.
Naumer, C. M., Fisher, K. E., & Dervin, B. (2008). Sense-making: A methodological perspective. *Proceedings of the SIGCHI Conference on Human Factors in Computing Systems* (pp. 506–513). Florence. Retrieved 24 February 2025, from https://www.researchgate.net/publication/238691238_Sense Making_A_Methodological_Perspective/citations
Riesman, D. (1951). Obiter dicta: The Nylon War. *ETC: A General Review of Semantics, 8*(3), 163–170.
Sartre, J.-P. (1948/1973). *Existentialism & Humanism.* London: Eyre Methuen.
Sartre, J.-P. (1957/1985). *Existentialism and Human Emotions.* New York: Citadel Press.
Singer, M. G. (1963). The Golden Rule. *Philosophy – The Journal of the Royal Institute of Philosophy, 38*(146), 293–314.
Thompson, C. J., Locander, W. B., & Pollio, H. R. (1990). The lived meaning of free choice: An existential-phenomenological description of everyday consumer experiences of contemporary women. *Journal of Consumer Research, 17*(December), 346–361.
Wahl, J. (1959/2019). *Philosophies of Existence: An Introduction to the Basic Thought of Kierkegaard, Heidegger, Jaspers, Marcel, Sartre.* Abingdon: Routledge.
Winnicott, D. W. (1989). *Playing and Reality.* London: Routledge.

Rethinking authenticity 6

Bring your whole self to work

In Shakespeare's *Hamlet*, Polonius offers his son Laertes a good many pithy proverbial sayings which persist in the English language to this day. In concluding his torrent of advice, he states, 'This above all: to thine own self be true. And it must follow, as the night the day, thou canst not then be false to any man' (Shakespeare, 1603/2007, p. 1935). This is clearly seen as vital not merely as a matter of personal principle but because it alters for the better how we then relate to others – and potentially how those others might then see us.

These days, if Polonius was a CEO delivering a litany of glib pronouncements at a corporate "town hall meeting", it is unlikely that his advice would be that we should be *true to oneself*, a statement that gives permission for the audience to embrace their personal freedom. Instead, he would be likely to invite everyone to bring their whole (or authentic) self to work.

The difference between these two approaches should be apparent: the former is respectful of those on whom the company relies, inviting them to enjoy a level of autonomy that would very likely feel immensely rewarding. It is a concession of power, a straightforward declaration that allows the CEO to helpfully cede some of their control by acknowledging that empowerment depends upon giving those around you the space and opportunity to embrace their own power, as opposed to a tiny package of power that can be safely delegated to them without dramatically affecting the overall dynamics.

DOI: 10.4324/9781003592624-6

The latter can be seen to be a managerialist instruction; we are told to bring everything about ourselves across the threshold of the business, not because it advantages us to have the distinction between our existence at work and in more personal settings but because an exposed "whole self" is potentially more susceptible to control in the workplace. This despite the fact that many businesses have craftily yoked together their public position on issues of inclusion in the workplace with a seemingly generous suggestion that all who are employed there can be an utterly unbridled and unconstrained version of themselves.

As is so often the case with such approaches, the public declarations that foreground diversity serve also to leave the system unchallenged and untouched, in terms of both its fundamental nature and in respect to how people actually experience this notional freedom, which can be described as follows:

> Imagine turning up at your new employer's team event to find you're the only one in formal attire – everyone else is in jeans and trainers. When you check the email later, you see it does indeed state formal – but your colleagues already knew to ignore it. The "in crowd" knew the hidden rules of the game. Something similar happens every time a person from a historically marginalised group joins a company that boldly claims: "We allow you to bring your whole self to work." The reality is often very different. You can bring your whole self to work but you can't be so obvious about your gender situation or so outspoken in meetings – or be quite so African American.
>
> (Peacock, 2022)

This observation provides rich insight into the systemic intolerance that denies everyone genuine scope to exercise their own power. It's not the "whole self" that is being enticed into the workplace – but a sanitised corporate version that is deemed to be culturally acceptable in that specific context. In that regard, we are back again facing down the presence of essentialist takes on personhood, with powerful people potentially working to graft their ideal image of a particular type of person onto those who come into work alongside them. To that extent, it is useful to revisit Barbara Banda's research into what she describes as "The Model Black", an essentialist perspective projected onto black people in the workplace in terms of who and how they should be when in that context. This involves adopting the dominant perspective and behaviours, self-silencing in the face of challenging circumstances, and actively softening their presence so as not to stand out in terms of the category of Other (Banda, 2022).

The business of turning up at work

Superficially, there is a notional commercial reason for why leaders fixate on this idea of the "whole self", which provides a rationale for this focus. Hence, it is argued that:

> The notion of the whole self variously captures the idea that people are more engaged in work if they believe in a firm's purpose; that teams are more effective if colleagues understand each other; that people with different identities should feel comfortable in their own skins; that firms should care about and respond to issues that affect their staff's well-being, from mental health to child care; and that leaders need to show some of their personal side to be connected with their staff.
>
> (Bartleby, 2022)

There may be an element of truth underlying every one of these assertions – but each represents an assumption which may be experienced very differently by both the leaders and their followers. Despite this, one of the major advocates of this asserts that our individual success at work depends on porting everything about ourselves into the workplace – and being prepared to make ourselves vulnerable in so doing. As ever with so many discussions about our experiences in corporate life, this fetishisation of vulnerability is discussed with no reference to the power dynamics of the organisations in which we find ourselves. It is also suggested that the success of our organisations is also dependent on everyone turning up as their "whole self", which is a somewhat manipulative position to assume: if you don't bring your whole self to work, the company – and hence your workmates – will suffer (Robbins, 2018).

For some, the whole argument is little more than a corporate deceit. In this regard, the entire workplace promotion of bringing your whole self to the workplace – something that invariably sits with the HR department in their role as the shock troops of managerialism – is argued to be:

> a cheap benefit — easier for employers to provide than, say, a raise — and one vague enough to be largely meaningless. Nor is it available to the majority of the American work force. Nobody is asking a line worker or customer service representative to add more personal vulnerability to the enterprise. For most gainfully employed people, it's not work's job to provide self-fulfillment or self-actualization. It's to put food on the table.
>
> (Paul, 2022)

This leads to the simple argument that we go into the workplace in order to work. I have to concede that my relationship to work for most of my 40-year career was purely instrumental: I turned up and did the best I could do, in order that I was given money and thereby enabled to live and enjoy my life in a capitalist system. It is only now – and after my most recent tenure in a salaried role – that I feel motivated by something other than the allure of the paycheck. For some people, this leads to the sensible argument that it is the parts of ourselves that contribute to effectiveness in the workplace – in terms of our own performance or that of the people that the structure notionally puts us in charge of – that we should bring with us over the threshold of the business. The rest should stay at home (Golden, 2021).

This leads to a conclusion that rather than the whole self, we would be better off focusing on bringing something called our *"role self"* into work (Bartleby, 2022). However, both concepts – whole and role – fly in the face of the existentialist notion that existence precedes essence, as they are categories that assume some level of fixed definition – and hence are constituted by a repertoire of explicit attitudes and behaviours to which we must aspire. It also leads us into a somewhat robotic and performative version of our presence in the workplace. In contrasting what are presumed to be two separate selves – a professional self that turns up at work and a privately personal self that may take a completely opposite view of the world – we end up in a situation where 'Pretending to be someone you are not is not a problem; it's essential' (Bartleby, 2022).

Human beings are not mix-and-match

In terms of engaging with the notion of self in a workplace context, it would seem for us all as human agents that there is a need to stop segmenting ourselves. We are not mere repositories of an array of insights and abilities upon which we can draw in order to offer a specific self to the range of circumstances that we find ourselves confronting. Such a view of our existence sees us as something akin to a floral bouquet: in some settings and at certain times that bouquet turns up as made up mostly of roses, a few sprays of greenery, and some lilies; meanwhile, on another occasion and in light of a different situation, the bouquet consists mostly of chrysanthemums and carnations.

But we are not like bouquets, determined and defined by the perceived needs of a particular context and the expectations of the people around us. We are thinking and acting existences in the world, living our lives in the moment – and blessed with freedom to look at that world and decide moment by moment how we choose to make our way through the time that we have in that world. The "pick-and-mix" model undergirds so much thinking in a business context, yet lacks humanity when you apply a critical analysis to it. For example, the conjoined artefacts of the Job Description and the Person Specification are crudely essentialist documents that dehumanise people and merely render them as constellations of experience, thinking, and practice. We seek to make ourselves fit that bureaucratic simplification of the social world, which denies our humanity.

The corporate activities that sit under the rubric of *talent management* operate in much the same way. I recall being actively involved in this at an organisation where I worked. The structure of this sort of work generates an idealised picture of a person – and, in light of that, does not merely seek out those who match that image but also tacitly encourages those who aspire to progression to actively adapt themselves to fit the profile that, in so many ways, has been arbitrarily generated. The process is justified in terms of its usefulness and effectiveness by the scientism that attends it, by which I mean the way in which it is rationalised through the profiling instruments used and the quantification deployed, which effectively effaces the humanity of those who are the objects of this activity: to use the vital distinction in terms of human relationships that Martin Buber so usefully offers, it is more *I-It* – a person relating to another as an object – than *I-Thou*, which is about individuals coming together in a shared subjectivity (Buber, 1937).

Elsewhere, a company called BetterUp is heavily focused on the "whole self" notion, which it underscores regularly in the blog posts on its website. In one article in this regard, it is observed that:

> Authenticity at work is when employees feel safe, secure, and comfortable showing up as their whole selves. To fully show up authentically, employees need a deep sense of belonging and psychological safety. But authenticity at work can be more complicated than it seems. There's a delicateness to showing up as your whole self. It takes heightened and intentional self-awareness and Inner Work® to show up authentically in the workplace.
>
> (Miles, 2022)

This begins well by seemingly making the case that shaping the workplace makes a huge difference to the experience of that environment of the workforce. But then we move rapidly into the idea that the individual needs to adjust themself in order to feel safe being themself at work. It sets people off chasing some fantasy notion of their essential self, the person notionally hidden behind a range of protective behaviours.

This is made explicitly clear in the post when the author makes the observation that 'To be authentic means that you are truly showing up as yourself. As defined in Merriam Webster, authentic means you are worthy of acceptance and true to your own personality' (Miles, 2022). Existentialism states categorically that there is no personality to which to be true: we emerge as a person thrown into the world solely in terms of the choices we make and the actions that we take. Anything else can be considered as another person's imposition upon us, to which we can, of course, choose to succumb to or expressly reject. This is an important illustration of the freedom that we enjoy in respect to our lives.

Existentialist authenticity

Existentialism as a way of seeing and being in the world rests on the key notion of acknowledged agency. In practice, this is seen to mean that 'selfhood is not naturally given but must be "won over" from a state of complacency, conformity, and self-forgetfulness' (Michelman, 2010, p. 43). It is about a life lived through activism as opposed to complicity. This foundational notion can be found in the work of Kierkegaard, Heidegger, and – of course – Sartre. Authenticity in this respect – as opposed to the somewhat glib notion of the concept that we have seen prevails in corporate life – is very much about the extent to which I embrace my finitude, freedom, and responsibility – or whether I am seen to be distancing myself from that position through immersing myself in self-distraction (Michelman, 2010, p. 43). And, in our contemporary society, there are a huge number of ways in which I can pass time instead of actively existing in it.

The element of choice is once again central here, as can be discerned in an analysis of Heidegger's thinking around authenticity, where it is argued that:

> Immersion in the social world … involves a certain abdication of selfhood. Immersed in the social world you do not *own* yourself, but rather you are "dispersed" in the social world. Heidegger contrasts such dispersal with self-ownership or authenticity …. Simply in virtue of being human, we face a choice of sorts between self-ownership and dispersal.
>
> (Blattner, 2024, p. 42)

Heidegger recognises that the business of being-in-the-world entails us being "ensnared" in that world and also that we interpret ourselves 'in terms of that world by its reflected light' (Heidegger, 1993a). This conspires, of course, to make being authentic all the more difficult. That said, as Viktor Frankl explains so powerfully in light of his experiences amongst others in the Nazi death camp at Auschwitz, 'everything can be taken from a man but one thing: the last of the human freedoms – to choose one's attitude in any given set of circumstances, to choose one's own way' (Frankl, 1946/2004, p. 75). Elsewhere, he noted that the neuroticism that was prevalent in general society seemed to completely fade away amongst the prisoners in the camp … and seemingly and somewhat surprisingly few caught up in this horror chose to take their own lives (Frankl, 2024, p. 36).

One way of understanding these observations is through an explicit recognition of how finding oneself in a concentration camp impacted those poor souls. It is suggested that they found themselves in a physical and social space in which the distractions of everyday life – specifically money, power, fame, and happiness – were no longer meaningfully present. Being denied these distractions saw the individual being reduced to their most basic presence in the world. Whilst these fascinations melted away in this context, it was also the case that:

> [S]imultaneously, the person himself had melted down, burned up by pain and seared through by suffering; melted right down to his very *being*. What had melted away was the *having*. One *has* money, one *has* power, one *has* fame, one *has* happiness; but one *is* a human being.
>
> (Frankl, 2024, p. 70) [Emphasis in original]

Living in a way that is authentic entails an interesting paradox in which the voice that is familiar to us contrasts with something in Heideggerian philosophy that gets called the *voice of conscience*. This is not the voice of God but the voice we might use in terms of accepting the responsibility to be free. However, the familiar voice is said to contrast with that which we might find ourselves using as and when we choose to choose. Hence, the latter has the potential to feel to us to be one that is most strange (Bakewell, 2016, p. 78). This is a reminder that we need to work at embracing our authenticity, as it is not something that flows automatically from simply finding oneself being in the world.

Thinking phenomenologically

It is also argued that anyone trying to live in a way that is mindful of existentialism is best suited to attend to their being in the world phenomenologically, which is an approach that focuses closely and tightly on describing the experience of living in the way in which it is experienced, which is as an embodied and reflective individual. This leads to the helpful conclusion that 'By describing experience well, he or she hopes to understand this existence and awaken us to ways of living more *authentic* lives' (Bakewell, 2016, p. 34) [Emphasis in original]. Phenomenology is a method of seeing the world from an immersion in it and can be defined as follows:

> It claims, first and foremost, to be a *radical* way of doing philosophy, a *practice* rather than a system. Phenomenology is best understood as a radical, anti-traditional style of philosophising, which emphasises the attempt to get to the truth of matters, to describe *phenomena*, in the broadest sense as whatever appears in the manner in which it appears, that is as it manifests itself to consciousness, to the experiencer. As such, phenomenology's first step is to seek to avoid all misconstructions and impositions placed on experience in advance, whether these are drawn from religious or cultural traditions, from everyday common sense, or, indeed, from science itself. Explanations are not to be imposed before the phenomena have been understood from within.
>
> (Moran, 2000, p. 4) [Emphasis in original]

Even with this seemingly simplified definition, it still seems arcane and impenetrable, in terms of how the world is seen and experienced through the lens of phenomenology. Yet philosophically it is an extremely useful way in which to engage with existence and all that comes together to make that up, as it looks to encourage us to immerse ourselves in day-to-day life rather than abstract ourselves from it. In light of this, I am going to share details of an experience that I had early in 2024 so as to provide a practical grounding for a more detailed exploration of what underpins this way of being.

Under the Wembley arch

On 5 May 2024, Bromley FC faced Solihull Moors in the National League play-off final, a football game that was played at Wembley stadium. Insofar as I consider Bromley to be my hometown, where to date I have lived around half of my life, I have always followed the football club there, whilst remaining a supporter of Charlton Athletic. This was a major event for Bromley FC, as never in their 132-year history had they ever played in the football league. The picture below shows where I sat for the match, just a few rows back from the pitch.

FIGURE 6.1 My seat at Wembley

As noted on several occasions in this book, our society is unhelpfully dominated by *scientism*, a view of the world that suggests that the scientific method is appropriate in terms of exploring and understanding all aspects of our life. Hence, it has been suggested that:

> The word "Scientism" … is to be understood as meaning the belief that science, in the modern sense of that term, and the scientific method as described by modern scientists, afford the only reliable natural means of acquiring such knowledge as may be available about whatever is real.
>
> (Wellmuth, 1944, pp. 1–2)

Elsewhere, six signs of scientism have been suggested as a further effort to define what is meant by this term, which are stated as:

1. Using the words "science," "scientific," "scientifically," "scientist," etc., honorifically, as generic terms of epistemic praise.
2. Adopting the manners, the trappings, the technical terminology, etc., of the sciences, irrespective of their real usefulness.

> 3. A preoccupation with demarcation, i.e., with drawing a sharp line between genuine science, the real thing, and "pseudo-scientific" imposters.
>
> 4. A corresponding preoccupation with identifying the "scientific method," presumed to explain how the sciences have been so successful.
>
> 5. Looking to the sciences for answers to questions beyond their scope.
>
> 6. Denying or denigrating the legitimacy or the worth of other kinds of inquiry besides the scientific, or the value of human activities other than inquiry, such as poetry or art.
>
> (Haack, 2012, pp. 77–78)

Hence, to look at Figure 6.1 above through the lens of scientism is to fundamentally reduce it to what can be seen. This form of visibility links closely to quantifiability: if I assert that I was sitting mostly amongst men at the game, there is a scientific imperative to evidence that in terms of substantiating the assertion through the use of figures. This might lead to the observation that, in the moment captured by the photograph, I am in close proximity to six men and what would appear to be at least one (and possibly two) women. Scientism fetishises the *factual*, so further analysis might lead to observations such as, whilst Wembley has three tiers of seating, only the lowest tier around the ground looked to be occupied. This might lead to pontification about the number of people actually in the stadium – potentially 50 per cent below capacity – or an act of triangulation, wherein the statements deriving from the picture are then tallied against other sources of information, such as the gate on the day.

A further interrogation of this picture shaped by scientism might highlight that the weather was dry on the day – or, at the very least, dry at the point at which this picture was taken. A line of inquiry could be suggested through consideration of this visual record as to why, when it was fine and the sky seemed bright and clear, the floodlights were on. To make sense of this would require further investigation, although a thesis could be advanced as to why this might have been the case, which would then need to be tested evidentially in some fashion.

It is important to state here that the scientific method is relevant in a good many circumstances wherein we are seeking to make sense of the world. However, as suggested above, it cannot apply in every possible circumstance – and other means of developing understanding exist that have a different foundation to that which underpins the scientific method. This leads to the sensible assessment that:

> It is one thing to celebrate science for its achievements and remarkable ability to explain a wide variety of phenomena in the natural world. But to claim there is nothing knowable outside the scope of science would be similar to a successful fisherman saying that whatever he can't catch in his nets does not exist. Once you accept that science is the only source of human knowledge, you have adopted a philosophical position (scientism) that cannot be verified, or falsified, by science itself. It is, in a word, unscientific.
>
> (Burnet, 2012)

Returning to the photograph of Wembley, I want now to speak phenomenologically about it, which will take us beyond merely trying to interpret the content scientifically and will thereby foreground the fact that I was present in that situation – and that my experience of being there and how I processed that at the time is as important as efforts to inscribe measurability on what can be seen in that picture. My human reactions to this set of circumstances, in light of my mental state, offer insight that is different to the capture and formalised presentation of quantified data but present a rich picture of the business of being in the world.

I was extremely eager to attend on that day in May but was still strongly experiencing the grip that Covid-related anxiety had on me, so I agonised about whether I could find the strength to attend this important match. As ever in these situations, I negotiated with myself that I would make arrangements to go, in terms of buying a ticket, but would decide at the very last minute whether to actually attend or not, depending on how I felt. It was clear to me early on that I would not be able to travel to Wembley via public transport, as I had only once or twice been on a train since the pandemic arrived in 2020 … and those short journeys took place at the quietest times of the day – and did not involve travelling into the capital. The pre-Covid memory of being crushed up against crowds on a busy Tube train filled me with dread, so I booked a parking space at a multistorey at the stadium and planned to drive in.

On that Sunday in 2024, I awoke in a slight state of panic. I visualised crowded spaces that I had experienced in the past, particularly those that arose out of sporting events, and considered how well I might cope with that sort of proximity on this occasion considering how I now saw the world and the risks therein. As I've said before, I relished lockdown, in light of my fragile mental state, and maintained a high level of personal isolation even as society at large loosened the constraints that had been put in place in the hope of preventing the spread of the disease.

The psychotherapist with whom I have been working has helped hugely with making sense of this, in that – as I have mentioned elsewhere – he argues soundly and from a strongly existentialist position that anxiety is not a pathology: it is, instead, at a deep level, a basic human reaction to the anguish that arises out of being thrown into the world and being faced there with the freedom to make choices. There is also a strong sense, at a slightly more superficial level, that anxiety is a mindful response to risks that present in our day-to-day lives – and that it is useful in that it prompts us to evaluate that risk and make a reasoned judgement in respect to how best to proceed.

To get to Wembley in a timely fashion and ready for a 3pm kick off, I needed to leave home in the car by no later than 12.45pm. In the hour preceding this point, I agonised in terms of desperately wanting to be present at this fabulous event – and feeling consumed by anxiety at being in the midst of it, considering how many others would be around me in that space. In a conversation with my wife, she suggested that I drove to the stadium and parked up; thereafter, I could make an assessment as to how do-able it was for me to then leave the car and make my way in. When I made the decision to follow this suggestion, I suddenly felt quite a lot of the anguish dissipate, a reminder perhaps that it is being confronted with our freedom and the associated expectation that we should make a choice that creates existential panic … and that making a decision lifts some of that pressure off us.

When I arrived, there was plenty of traffic around, yet the multistorey car park seemed pleasingly quiet. I parked up and promptly stepped out of the car, then walking down the stairs to the level where I needed to come off in order to access the stadium. There were people around, of course, but no crushing crowds, although there was a small and tightly packed queue at the turnstiles which caused me a moment of hesitation and almost sent me scuttling back to the insulation of my car's cabin. Instead, I found the strength to ride it out … and entered a low ceilinged and extremely busy communal area behind the seating, where there were food and drink concessions and some toilets. Choices were clearly being made all the way and at every moment.

I made my way to my seat and took the picture that appears in Figure 6.1. I was extremely aware of being closer to other humans who I did not actually know than I had been for several years. I worked hard to focus out to a point in the middle of the pitch, so as not to dwell on the fact that people were alongside, ahead of, and behind me. It was busy but not oppressively slow … and my choice of seat, with just a couple of rows ahead of me and the touchline within easy distance, meant that I could avoid focusing on the busyness of where I was and the fact that we were all tightly packed together. Even the fact that a nice character in the seat to my right was chatty about the game and kept turning to speak to me face to face felt manageable. Despite the fact that I felt his breath wafting over my face in a way that made my nerves jangle in terms of the way I had ended up thinking of the world as being full of viral vectors (of which I, of course, could quite easily be one), I felt committed to sticking with the experience by this point, notwithstanding what might now come my way.

As I sat behind the scene that appears in that photograph, I felt ambivalent. On the one hand, I was full of joy at having got past my concerns and now being part of a thrilling event, a rich shared experience when I had banished such activity from my life over the course of the previous nigh on four years. But, on the other hand, I remained intensely mindful of where I was and how there was a real chance of catching Covid in such circumstances.

Ultimately, though, as the existence of the photo demonstrates, I was able to derive deep pleasure from being there, even when – after extra time had been played and the game went to penalties, which saw Bromley win promotion to League Two – the stands erupted and I started to get overwhelmed by a feeling of claustrophobia and my fear of crowds began to assert itself. For a moment, I considered running away, pushing my way past all of the people that had suddenly appeared around me. But another feeling flooded me at the same time, namely one of great joy and not wanting to miss being part of this massive celebration.

The happiness that washed over me briefly undid me and I found myself tearful as I watched the Bromley players receiving plaudits from the crowd all the way around the ground. I was also reminded of my late father's observation that he made regularly over many years that a town like Bromley should have had a football side in the league. I recall a flash of melancholy as I thought to myself, "Oh, I wish you were here to see this, Pop!" This also left me feeling weepy, of course!

Ways of seeing the world

I hope that this example offers some insight into how scientific approaches to making sense of the world provide one narrow way of capturing data in that regard – and can often be seen to deny other ways of assessing that experience. Scientism – the pre-eminent approach to data capture and manipulation – is dominant in our corporate settings and can often be seen to be reducing human beings to crude aggregates and categories. That focus on quantifiable measurability has another important effect, as well: it serves to silence people in terms of denying them the chance to engage with the world phenomenologically and find ways to share the richness of the insights that they derive from experiencing their world in that way.

For example, a staff survey reduces multiple rich and complex existences to a crudely aggregated quantity; the social power of numbers then denies the voices that contributed to that figure, in terms of the actual existential experiences of that range of individuals. The numbers are privileged and prioritised, while the actuality of people living through specific circumstances is condemned to silence. We fetishise numbers, a seemingly simple act which – in turn – relegates voice firmly to the background, where it is not at all properly or honestly heard.

It is important to hold in mind that phenomenology "is a matter of describing, not of explaining or analysing. Husserl's first directive to phenomenology, in its early stages, to be a 'descriptive psychology', or to return to the 'things themselves', is from the start a foreswearing of science' (Merleau-Ponty, 1945/2005, p. ix). Clearly, the idea of taking our experience of the world and finding ways by which to describe it stands a long way from the supposed rigour of the scientific method. But that robustness is self-referential – and cannot be allowed to erase the importance of listening to our own experiences – and to the articulations of their experiences by others. In far too many cases, the data-filled spreadsheet acts as a gag that stifles voice and denies people the chance to speak and be heard.

To make sense of the workplace might involve some statistical data and some aggregation of people's experiences so as to potentially identify overarching themes ... but this is interpretive work, which may involve dominant voices notionally speaking on behalf of others, whereas we need also to make space for descriptive voices – which we need to hear not in order to interpret but instead to help us understand the experiences of others.

In terms of making sense of the richness that Merleau-Ponty brings to this understanding of how it is to engage with our lives in this personalised way, the following summary of his four themes is helpfully suggested:

> The aim of phenomenology is *description* of phenomena. Phenomena include anything that appears or presents itself such as feelings, thoughts and objects. *Reduction* is a process that involves suspending or bracketing the phenomena so that the "things themselves" can be returned to. An *essence* is the core meaning of an individual's experience that makes it what it is. Finally, *intentionality* refers to consciousness and individuals are always conscious of something.
>
> (Ehrich, 2005) [Emphasis added]

There are two phenomenological formulations, a distinction requiring acknowledgement here without getting too embroiled in this somewhat arcane discussion: one is called *descriptive* – which derives from the work of Husserl – and the other is referred to as *interpretive*, which is how Heidegger envisages the practice. The former sought to set aside pre-conceived ideas and to focus in on our actual conscious experience of the world. The latter aims to define our experience of the world by incorporating existing views of our world. It is suggested that Heidegger's approach actively embraces hermeneutics, the philosophy of interpretations, which 'moves beyond the description or core concepts of the experience and seeks meanings that are embedded in everyday occurrences' (Reiners, 2012).

The descriptive approach encourages us to immerse ourselves in our experiences without being too concerned about imposing meaning on them. This leads to an expectation that we bracket off extant ideas about our circumstances and do not allow our experience to be influenced by that. It sets aside analytic thinking in favour of recognising the richness of our presence in the world, which Husserl described thus:

> I find myself at all times, and without my ever being able to change this, set in relation to a world which, through its constant changes, remains one and ever the same. It is continually "present" for me, and I myself am a member of it. Therefore this world is not there for me as a mere world of *facts and affairs*, but, with the same immediacy, as a *world of values*, a *world of goods*, a *practical world*. Without further effort on my part I find the things before me furnished not only with the qualities that befit their positive nature, but with value-characters such as beautiful or ugly, agreeable or disagreeable, pleasant or unpleasant, and so forth.
>
> (Husserl, 1931/2012, p. 53) [Emphasis in original]

By way of contrast, the interpretive orientation refutes the idea that there is value in denying pre-existing understanding. In terms of the philosophy that undergirds this, it is argued that 'hermeneutics goes beyond mere description of core concepts and essences to look for meanings embedded in common life practices' (Lopez & Willis, 2004).

By way of a summary of how best to think about phenomenology – and its intimate relationship with the idea of existentialist authenticity – it is a way of being in the world that doesn't seek to create a distance between the person and their existence. Far too often, when people speak about personal reflection, it ends up as quite abstracted; it is as if the person is able to remove themselves from the warp and weft of being and look at the world as if they were not part of it. This is why the distinction between reflection and reflexivity is so important. And it is also why phenomenology is essential to our authentic presence in the world, in that it 'focuses on consciousness and the content of conscious experience, such as judgments [sic], perceptions, and emotions' (Connelly, 2010, p. 127).

It is also noteworthy that we experience our lives as embodied beings as opposed to mere intellects floating around in the ether. Lastly, phenomenology is said to '...want to know what the experience was like to live it, not just the person's reaction to the experience' (ibid). Hence, to return to the exposition about choosing how we think about the world summarised in Figure 5.1, it is apparent that a phenomenological approach needs to undergird the way of actively engaging with the practicalities of existing that is outlined there.

To finish, it is worth noting in passing that phenomenology also informs some people's thinking in terms of how to conduct research in the world. Beneath that overarching picture sits a research practice which has come to be called *micro-phenomenology*. A leading thinker in this field asserts the idea behind micro-phenomenology is to tap into the unrecognised part of experience, which

> is what we call the "how" of experience: how we experience something. We usually focus on the "what," the content of an experience. For instance: "Oh, this sound is a bird's song," or "This shape is a tree," these are contents. In the same way, the experience of having an idea is almost always described in terms of the content of the idea. We are not aware of the experience involved in recognising this as a tree, a bird, or an idea. Shifting to the "how," we inquire for instance: what is my way of paying attention to the bird song, how did I come up with an idea, how do I experience the content I know, how did it emerge? Can I describe how am I experiencing this, in addition to describing what I am experiencing? How do I experience an idea, beyond its linguistic description, its content described verbally? Where is its meaning, is it in the words?
>
> (Petitmengin, 2025, p. 120)

This offers insight into the existential conundrum in which we find ourselves so much of the time, wherein we are firmly located in the world and are immersed in that experience. This existence requires of us that we take time to recognise where we are, so that we can live our life through a commitment to being aware of our presence in the world as a moment-by-moment experience in which we are compelled to recognise that we need to make decisions. Unfortunately, we find ourselves surrounded by a worldview that looks to scientise the life that we live. This adherence to the scientific method could in that respect be seen as a prime example of bad faith and existential inauthenticity, as we seek solace in an approach that objectifies the world and creates an illusory distance between us and it. In that regard, it offers comfort in terms of allowing us to manage our existential angst by creating a separation between our life and an interpretation of that life.

If engaging in the world through this abstract perspective is indeed a means by which we can turn away from the absurdity of life and evade our freedom in that context, then embracing phenomenology will be unsettling – but it will serve to put us more directly in contact with our existence. It is arguable that scientism actually closes off a large area of our experience to us, as can be seen in respect to this observation:

> Whether we are touching, seeing, listening, imagining, remembering, understanding or deciding, whether we are performing a concrete or an abstract activity, a large part of this activity, although lived through subjectively, is not immediately accessible to reflective consciousness and verbal description. We experience it, but in an unrecognized, unnoticed or pre reflective way. The most surprising thing is that we are not aware of this deficit of awareness, which is the first obstacle in the way of becoming conscious of this unrecognized part. However this difficulty of access does not mean that our lived experience is out of reach. It means that accessing it requires a particular expertise, which must be acquired.
>
> (Petitmengin et al., 2019, p. 694)

Getting to grips with the phenomenon of work

I open this section that looks to locate the discussion thus far about the challenge of authenticity in an existential sense and the need to embrace phenomenology in terms of meaningfully engaging with the world with a slab of what I take to be traditionalist ideology about the world of business and the organisations therein. The quote below is lifted from a monstrous tome of 2018 pages, packed full of guidance as to how to navigate the world of business. A riffle through its content offers immediate insight into how business tends to be thought about and what practices are deemed to be important. For example, there are extensive sections in this work covering topics such as *Strategy & Competition*; *Marketing*; *Finance*; and *Productivity*.

The quote comes from a commissioned essay looking at contemporary management.

> The practice of management, through both its scientific standards and its artistic renderings, remains the best way yet to channel the raw energy of human minds, the brute force of vast capital, and the quixotic capability of new technology to transform people by reshaping their perceptions of what's possible on this planet, and ultimately, even beyond.
>
> (Brown, 2006, p. 8)

Science and silence

The first noteworthy thing about the quote is the early declaration that management is distinguished by an adherence to scientific principles. Obviously, some managerial practice will draw upon activity that might be described as scientific, such as the statistical underpinnings of some of the ways that exist to manage finances. However, as noted previously, foregrounding a scientific interpretation serves only to discursively render some elements of organisational life as beyond debate – you can't question the science, it's deemed to be an incontestable truth – and hence this labelling creates a mechanism that serves to silence difference of opinion and dissent in terms of corporate direction.

Promoting the idea that scientific method is fundamental to competent managerial practice does not merely close off the possibility of debate; it reinforces this by limiting the people able to contribute to such discussions to a select group who have been inducted into that corpus of knowledge and array of techniques. To engage in discussion about key aspects of business practice requires one to be steeped in a particular tradition of how to measure and manage the world … but, at the same time, the reliance of that tradition on a scientific approach sees the conclusions that arise from its application as simply beyond question.

Meanwhile, while the top of the organisation fixates on a particular sort of data – especially that expressed in a numeric format – and privileges it in terms of dialogue within that business space, the experiences of the vast majority of people who sustain the company in terms of its production and promotion of goods and services are denied, particularly when they are expressed personally and potentially phenomenologically. There are instances in organisational life when many of us can end up feeling that the scientific representation of the existing circumstances runs counter to our actual existential experiences. Yet we find it difficult then to challenge the situations that the data suggests exist, not because that information is robust and persuasive but simply because the way in which it is produced and presented is allowed to occupy a dominant position, particularly in a corporate setting.

I will take a moment here to reinforce the essential distinction between *science* – and the huge benefits that this has brought to the world (although its application in a specific socio -economic context can also be seen to have created problems) – and *scientism*. The latter is an ideological perspective on the scientific method that privileges it in each and every circumstance and can be seen to render the outputs of science as beyond question and contestation.

It also intimates that science is always right, whereas the reality is that science as a body of knowledge and practice is constantly evolving, a situation brilliantly illustrated by Thomas Kuhn's work on paradigm shifts, points in history when the accepted view of the world undergoes a shift in light of fresh scientific insight (Kuhn, 1970). This is perhaps best illustrated by the change to a heliocentric view of our solar system when previously the Earth was said to be at its centre.

The (abstract) art of management

Calling upon the idea that management can be thought of as an artful practice as we see in the ideological statement above seems to hint at the Aristotelian understanding of *episteme* and *techne*, a distinction that often ends up simplified into a crude distinction between knowledge and practice. However, careful attention to classical discussion about these two terms suggests that they are closely interrelated and that each informs the other: episteme is described as potentially both pure and applied science, whilst applied science seen through the lens of techne is understood as craft or art (Parry, 2024). All of which is best understood as follows: 'Episteme denotes "understanding of a matter," or more generally, knowledge: techne on the other hand suggests action, namely art, skill, or workmanship, something not only conceived, but knowledge going into action' (Rawlins, 1950), pp. 389–390.

It is entirely possible to read the particular text about the practice of management that I am exploring here at face value. The alternative is to have in mind as we engage with this statement the idea of *deconstruction*, which derives from a number of philosophers but is largely said to arise from the work of Jacques Derrida (Norris, 1991). While there is a tendency to try and define deconstruction as a method, it does not lend itself well to that. Instead, it is an intrinsic quality of any text that we might find ourselves reading, particularly if we approach it as something with which we are unfamiliar even if it is a piece that we see every day (Rolfe, 2004). It requires that we suspend our presuppositions and understandings in respect to what we are reading – and read it afresh, whilst allowing the text itself to unravel and, in so doing, reveal what might be seen to be occurring under its surface.

One commentator offers three precepts that might usefully undergird our approach to reading a text in this way: first, it is suggested that we should 'Think of such things as "the classroom", "the child", "the researcher" with invisible quotation marks around them: they are not "natural", not self-evident and never innocent' (Berman & MacLure, 2005, p. 286). Such terms patently have a deeper meaning woven into them, oftentimes operating at a tacit level for the audience of readers. It requires that we isolate these concepts and reflect on all of the meaning that is written into them.

Secondly, it is about being mindful in regard to the constructs that exist as assumptions in the textual context. In particular, it is suggested that we might usefully 'Look for the binary oppositions in texts … and worry away at them' (Berman & MacLure, 2005, p. 286). This is where we experience unquestioned either/or formulations, which often show up as an unspoken but experienced distinction between *Normalcy* and *Otherness*.

Lastly, we need to suspend our familiarity with the various observations, concepts, and ideas that appear and which structure our view of the world. This means looking more closely at anything that is deemed to be commonsensical, consensual, and uncontested, or is part of a routine in which we find ourselves immersed. This can be summarised thus, in terms of how we should engage with the text: 'Challenge the taken-for-granted – not in a destructive spirit, nor in the hope that you will reveal some deeper truth' (Berman & MacLure, 2005, p. 286). It is merely a matter of questioning dominant views of the world, as opposed to replacing them with an alternative yet similar picture in terms of its effect.

It is worth noting that Derrida's philosophy is seen to actively contest phenomenology, despite that perspective and deconstruction arising out of a relationship with the thought of Husserl. Derrida's post-structuralist assertion that everything is text and that there is no world outside of that context flies in the face of phenomenology's commitment to engaging with the world through one's embodied presence therein (Moran, 2000, p. 453). Nevertheless, setting aside that arcane discussion, there is virtue in my view to bearing in mind how we might read the world through a deconstructive lens without losing sight of the actual reality of our day-to-day existence. Zealots on both sides of the fence will contest this, but I am content with considering how two perspectives can be rendered hybrid in terms of supporting human beings to make sense of and critique their worlds.

Hence, returning to the defining statement in respect of management, the use of the term "art" carries substantial meaning when considering who should manage and how should they do it. If we allow this notion to unravel in the context in which it is being used, it would seem that it is intimating that only those with a particular talent – able in light of this to embrace a specific although undescribed craft – can be considered to be managers.

Additionally, the text makes a link between the capacity to engage with the world scientifically and the ability to apply that understanding to the actuality of life. In that sense, it limits even further those who might be considered capable of undertaking corporate management.

Said to be best, but what of the rest?

This textual item also asserts that management is the best means by which to undertake key activities in a business organisation. Once again, we need to consider this as it appears in the statement and allow the deconstruction of the text that occurs as we read it to posit the question in respect to binaries in the discussion: how does the presumption that this is the best way to achieve these ambitions impact other perspectives that might exist regarding organisational life but are being silenced by this assertion?

Technophilia

Finally, the deconstructive reading of this definitional piece sees the general notion of technology as positive in respect to its impact on the human beings around it. This common-sense observation may or may not be true, depending on the context in which it arises. However, it carries with it the strong sense of a particular agenda, one that may not be experienced in that way by people other than the author. The suggestion that technology stands alongside humankind and provokes a positive response is problematic because it can be seen as both a *means to an end* and *a human activity*; according to Heidegger, the two terms belong together because 'to posit ends and procure and utilize the means to them is a human activity' (Heidegger, 1993b, p. 312).

Rethinking work, and the why and how we do it

In the workplace, there are three sets of people who shape and define how we experience our existence in that environment: first, there are those charged with the responsibility of managing and leading the organisation; second, there are those around us, in terms of colleagues, peers, and direct reports; and lastly there are ourselves, in terms of how we choose to live our life at work. It is in the latter regard that the importance of existentialist authenticity emerges. However, that authenticity extends to all aspects of our life, so applies equally to how an individual navigates every element of their corporate presence, regardless of their position in the firm. Authenticity is a shared human issue, regardless of the essentialist definitions behind which we sometimes seek to hide ourselves, particularly in the workplace.

As we consider our authentic lives and seek to live in good faith, it is apparent that – if we are part of the management – we need to think and act in ways that look to offer everyone around us a positive opportunity to be like that in the world. This means finding ways to be confident about surrendering control so that people can experience their own freedom and make their own choices. In fact, creating those conditions should be seen as a key attribute of living authentically, not as a "leader" but as a human being. Our lives should be lived in liberty – and with the aim of liberating others.

Similarly, it is seen to be acting in good faith to support those around us to live authentically, which requires us to acknowledge the fact that people should be able to engage with the world in a way that leaves them feeling existentially content. And, lastly, we need to find ways in which to live our lives in a way that feels genuine and right as we navigate our way through the challenge of being thrown into the world – and partially landing in organisational life and the issues that arise therein.

To this end, it is important to hold in mind that our existence can also be seen as an act of resistance. To be oneself is to reject the labels that others seek to apply to us … but that entails taking up the responsibility for living our lives as we want to. Hence, in considering our embrace of phenomenology as a way of thinking about our experience, the following observation strikes me as extremely powerful:

> Whether it concerns caring for others or cultivating the land, doing research or building houses, entering into intimate contact with one's own experience is an act of liberation and resistance. Within all human activities, it is urgent to create, between the stitches of the tightly woven fabric of rules, constraints and strained schedules that inhibit

> this contact, joyful spaces of resistance: spaces where, together, we allow ourselves to slow down, to breathe, to listen to the felt dimension that animates our lives, to let new visions and new stories emerge from it, to imagine new ways of doing things, demonstrating here and now that they are possible. It is time to regain our life forces, to give meaning to our lives, and in doing so, give up the hope of controlling everything, of knowing everything, not even knowing if one day the multiplication of these spaces will burst the fabric.
>
> (Petitmengin, 2021, p. 179)

This, then, is how we might embrace a life lived in good faith. Yet it would seem that contemporary workplaces are not places where value is placed on the idea of slowing down and taking time to think about our existence. In that sense, to run counter to the dominant notions that exist within organisational life is indeed a major – and vitally important – act of resistance. Megan Reitz and John Higgins exquisitely state the challenge that we face in terms of seeking to be authentic in the workplace:

> We have become adept at relating to our world in a 'doing mode'; we attend to action, often focusing through a narrow, fragmented, instrumental lens of short-term productivity onto targets, metrics, agendas and to-do lists. This is a vital capacity for survival. It is, however, our contention … that, whilst we couldn't live without this mode, its value to us and our society is deeply dependent on us also being able to employ what we call a 'spacious mode', characterised by an expansive, exploratory attention where dynamic interdependencies and relationships are foregrounded and where, in the absence of pressure from immediate expectations, a different quality of insight becomes possible.
>
> (Reitz & Higgins, 2025, p. 5)

Bibliography

Bakewell, S. (2016). *At The Existentialist Cafe: Freedom, Being & Apricot Cocktails*. London: Chatto & Windus.

Banda, B. (2022). *The Model Black: How Black British Leaders Succeed in Organisations and Why It Matters*. Abingdon: Routledge.

Bartleby. (2022, June 14). Do not bring your whole self to work. Retrieved 26 February 2025, from *The Economist*: https://www.economist.com/business/2022/06/14/do-not-bring-your-whole-self-to-work

Berman, E., & MacLure, M. (2005). Deconstruction as a method of research. In B. Somekh, & C. Lewin, *Research Methods in the Social Sciences* (pp. 284–292). Thousand Oaks, CA: Sage.

Blattner, W. (2024). *Heidegger's Being and Time* (2nd ed.). London: Bloomsbury Academic.

Brown, T. (2006). Management in the 21st century. In B. Publishing, *Business: The Ultimate Resource* (pp. 6–9). London: A & C Black & Co.

Buber, M. (1937). *I and Thou*. Edinburgh: T & T Clark.

Burnet, T. (2012, 21 May). What is scientism? Retrieved 10 March 2025, from American Association of the Advancement of Science: *Dialogue on Science, Ethics and Religion*: https://sciencereligiondialogue.org/resources/what-is-scientism/

Connelly, L. M. (2010). What is phenomenology? *MEDSURG Nursing, 19*(2), 127–128.

Ehrich, L. (2005, 13 December). Revisiting phenomenology: Its potential for management research. Retrieved 10 March 2025, from QUT ePrints: https://eprints.qut.edu.au/2893

Frankl, V. E. (1946/2004). *Man"s Search for Meaning: The Classic Tribute to Hope from the Holocaust*. London: Rider.

Frankl, V. E. (2024). *Embracing Hope: On Freedom, Responsibility and the Meaning of Life*. London: Rider.

Golden, G. (2021, 9 April). Why it's a bad idea to bring your whole self to work. Retrieved February 2025, from *Psychology Today*: https://www.psychologytoday.com/gb/blog/curating-your-life/202104/why-it-s-bad-idea-bring-your-whole-self-work

Haack, S. (2012). Six signs of scientism. *Logos & Episteme, III*(I), 75–95.

Heidegger, M. (1993a). Being and Time: Introduction. In M. Heidegger, & D. F. Krell (Ed.), *Basic Writings –(*Revised and Expanded ed.) (pp. 37–87). London: Routledge.

Heidegger, M. (1993b). The question concerning technology. In M. Heidegger, & D. F. Krell (Ed.), *Basic Writings* (Revised and Expanded ed.) (pp. 311–341). London: Routledge.

Husserl, E. (1931/2012). *Ideas: General Introduction to Pure Phenomenology*. Abingdon: Routledge.

Kuhn, T. S. (1970). *The Structure of Scientific Revolutions* (2nd ed.). Chicago: University of Chicago Press.

Lopez, K. A., & Willis, D. G. (2004). Descriptive Versus Interpretive Phenomenology: Their Contributions to Nursing Knowledge. *Qualitative Health Research, 14*(5), 726–735.

Merleau-Ponty, M. (1945/2005). *Phenomenology of Perception*. London: Routledge.

Michelman, S. (2010). *The A to Z of Existentialism*. Lanham, MD: The Scarecrow Press.

Miles, M. (2022, March 14). Why is authenticity at work so hard? 5 ways to be more authentic. Retrieved 27 February 2025, from BetterUp: https://www.betterup.com/blog/authenticity-at-work

Moran, D. (2000). *Introduction to Phenomenology*. London: Routledge.

Norris, C. (1991). *Deconstruction*. London: Routledge.

Parry, R. (2024, 19 December). Episteme and techne (E. N. Zalta, & U. Nodelman, Eds.). Retrieved 13 March 2025, from *The Stanford Encyclopedia of Philosophy*: https://plato.stanford.edu/archives/win2024/entries/episteme-techne

Paul, P. (2022, 25 September). Do not bring your whole self to work. Retrieved 26 February 2025, from *The New York Times*: https://www.nytimes.com/2022/09/25/opinion/business-economics/work-office-whole-self.html

Peacock, A. (2022, 28 April). How to turn the "bring your whole self to work" myth into workplace reality. Retrieved 26 February 2025, from *HR Magazine*: https://www.hrmagazine.co.uk/content/comment/how-to-turn-the-bring-your-whole-self-to-work-myth-into-workplace-reality

Petitmengin, C. (2021). Anchoring in lived experience as an act of resistance. *Constructivist Foundations, 16*(2), 172–181.

Petitmengin, C. (2025). Micro-phenomenology as coming into contact with experience: Subtilisation, surprises, and liberation. In D. Schoeller, S. Thorgeirsdottir, & G. Walkerden, *Practicing Embodied Thinking in Research and Learning* (pp. 119–128). Abingdon: Routledge.

Petitmengin, C., Remillieux, A., & Valenzuela-Moguillansky, C. (2019). Discovering the structures of lived experience: Towards a micro-phenomenological analysis method. *Phenomenology and the Cognitive Sciences, 18*, 691–730.

Rawlins, F. I. (1950). Episteme and techne. *Philosophy and Phenomenological Research, 10*(3), 389–397.

Reiners, G. M. (2012). Understanding the differences between Husserl's (descriptive) and Heidegger's (interpretive) phenomenological research. *Journal of Nursing and Care, 1*(5). Retrieved 11 March 2025, from https://www.hilarispublisher.com/open-access/understanding-the-differences-husserls-descriptive-and-heideggers-interpretive-phenomenological-research-2167-1168.1000119.pdf

Reitz, M., & Higgins, J. (2025). *Permisson to Pause: Rediscovering ';Spaciousness' at Work*. Retrieved from *Megan Reitz*: https://static1.squarespace.com/static/597729cbcf81e0f87c7f6c61/t/677b9b9a26a22a7351dce717/1736154022120/SpaciousnessREPORT_90pp_FULL.pdf

Robbins, M. (2018). *Bring Your Whole Self to Work: How Vulnerability Unlocks Creativity, Connection, and Performance.* Carlsbad, CA: Hay House.
Rolfe, G. (2004). Deconstruction in a nutshell. *Nursing Philosophy, 5*(3), 274–276.
Shakespeare, W. (1603/2007). *Hamlet.* In J. Bate, & E. Rasmussen (Eds.), *William Shakespeare: Complete Works* (p. 1935). Basingstoke: Macmillan.
Wellmuth, J. (1944). *The Nature and Origins of Scientism.* Milwaukee, WI: Marquette University Press.

7 Living our lives at work mindfully

The reason I began to explore the world of work from an existentialist perspective was a sudden recognition of just how much of my life had been spent there. However, it was not just the amount of time that this activity had consumed, equating to 40 years of my life in which I spent 37 or so hours a week (of around 45 weeks of the year, once leave is taken out) doing not what I truly wanted to do but what I had to do. It was the way in which I ended up unquestioningly immersed in this pursuit. Moreover, the pressure of having to work, in terms of undertaking paid employment, seemed for most of that time to prevent me from even taking a moment to consider what I would truly have liked to spend that time doing.

As I stepped away from salaried employment, I felt two emotions. Primarily, there was an enormous sense of freedom in suddenly not having to comply any more with the constraining expectations and structures of the workplace and – at the same time – a sense of anxiety, as I suddenly came to realise that how I chose to live my life was now entirely down to me. In the latter regard, I suddenly saw how dependent I had been on a formal working life, in terms of giving me shape and direction. This revelation meant that it suddenly felt as though, up until that point, my life had not been my own. Instead, it had been shaped, controlled and directed by others and by the expectations of the ways in which we have ended up working in our society – and the socio-economic system that determines that.

My initial reaction to this insight was a rush of despair. We are all of us trapped in this structure. There is an option to go "off grid" but that is an individual choice that leaves our existing circumstances unquestioned and unchanged. How could I have lived my life differently considering how the world seeks to compel us to live? What ways could I have taken to step away

DOI: 10.4324/9781003592624-7

from acquiescence and find the inner capacity to take responsibility for my life, when everyone's lives look to be defined outside of themselves?

This coincided with my time with Malcolm, exploring the grip on me that the anxiety that had initially arisen in response to the appearance of Covid-19 was having. Suddenly, some of the key notions that underpin existentialism became ways in which to see my world differently – and to frame ways of being in that world in a way that felt more as though I was in control.

This final section revisits the concepts that I have explored in Chapters 1–6 in order to openly discuss how they can be used to think about our lives at work and hopefully change them for the better. This is undertaken at two levels: first, how can I live my own life at work in a way that feels honest to me; and, second, if I have responsibility for the running of the workplace, how can I manage and lead in that context in a way that seeks to maximise the opportunity for those around me to live an honest life? This is not a programme of action. Instead, the observations in this chapter seek to prompt each and every one of us to think deeply about our lives and how we would like to live them … and also about our relationships with others as we all come together in the world, and try and make our way through it.

Chapter 1: The business of being

The workplace is full of labels and titles. At first glance, these look to be simply descriptors, but they are actually experienced as the imposition of ways of being. It is all part of how our lives are endlessly categorised. I concede that some would argue that this codified framing is the only way in which we can understand the world; the existentialist view would be that we should focus less on that sort of understanding of the world and more on how we all actively make the world by our presence in it.

Those labels and titles are artificial constructs, which seem to offer templates for being to which we are expected to aspire. For example, the post to which you are appointed in a company has both a formal and a cultural way of being seen: the former appears as a job description and a person specification, the latter as the tacit expectations in the organisation for what that role is expected to deliver and how it is expected to do it.

In both cases, the rigidity of this approach denies your capacity as a human being simply to be in the world and to navigate your way through it. It ends up being a role that you are being expected to play, rather than an opportunity for you to actively live your life in a workplace setting and make a difference as a result. It takes us back to Sartre's foundational principle of existentialism, namely that existence precedes essence. First and foremost, we need to live our lives … and, in so doing, the way in which we choose to do that defines us as a person and – to an extent – contributes to a collective definition of humanity, albeit one that is constantly in a state of flux. We do not occupy a role; rather, we create the role around us by our presence in the world and how we might find our way through it.

> *So, as an individual …*
> Don't be defined by the labels of life. Define yourself through living your life.
> *And, as someone who has positional power to impact on others around you …*
> Think of the world as made up of people and not simply of roles and labels. An existentialist approach focuses on the vitality of being *human* and not on the idea of being a *resource*.

At an even deeper level, there is a need to maintain our focus on our being a human agent rather than a being in the workplace. As we have discussed, we have a limited time in this world, an observation that – as we have seen through the work of Kierkegaard – applies equally whether or not one has a faith and a religion. There is a need to focus on our life and not on the promise of an afterlife … and, in so doing, one powerful question appears which every one of us needs to take time to answer:

> *As a person, ask yourself this …*
> Is this how I want to spend the time that I have … and, if not, how would I prefer to spend it?
> *And, if you have power over how others experience work, the question is …*
> How can I work with those around me to make the environment in which we are collectively living our lives as engaging and meaningful as possible?

To ask oneself these types of question is to open the door to a deep sense of anxiety … and to embrace that as not necessarily a pathology – although it can end up being experienced as an illness, of course – but as a key feature of being in the world. Sometimes the organisational hierarchy in which we find ourselves working can help us to avoid confronting those things that existentialism argues create the anguish of being alive. I spent years at work avoiding that angst by tricking myself into thinking that everything that was happening around me was the result of the actions of others. Latterly, I was compelled to embrace that anxiety, as I recognised that – without acknowledging the fact – I had chosen to live my life in a particular way but had not taken responsibility for that.

Wherever we find ourselves in the workplace, it is important to concede that we need to actively engage with the responsibility of being in the world. We are thrown into the situation where we find ourselves but thereafter must recognise our freedom to make choices, rather than delude ourselves – as I did for many years – that we are forced to face constraints derived from structures and the expectations of others around us … and have no choice but to succumb to that.

The keystone choice that holds up the workplace structure around us is superficially simple and yet complex: do I choose to live my life or do I inhabit a life that has been chosen for me? Am I content to spend a large chunk of my time in the world working in the way that I have experienced to date – or do I want to live that life differently? It's important to recall here that it is the act of choosing that matters existentially rather than the radicality of the decision that we make. Even if one chooses to continue to live at work in a way that sees you defined by an externally imposed label or where you opt not to try to live your life differently, it is the case that some thought has gone into the living of a life, as opposed to distracting oneself from the reality in which one finds oneself.

Chapter 2: Free to work, or free to be free

Being responsible for creating myself from nothing, as existentialism suggests, is a massive responsibility. Being me rests exclusively on my shoulders … and I cannot blame anyone else for the me that I might be across the course of my time in the world. For example, I might find myself blaming my poor mum and dad for my ongoing lack of confidence and ambition. Certainly, my immediate family would quickly and pointedly denigrate someone who was seen as being "too full of themselves". My mother's favourite way of articulating this would be to openly suggest that someone had "eye trouble", which would initially leave you wondering what might be wrong with their sight. When quizzed further about this, she would explain with a smile that "All you ever hear them saying is "I" did this, "I" did that, "I" am good at this, "I" have done well … they've got "I", "I", "I" trouble!"

This was a feature of growing up in my family … but I had a clear choice as to whether to subscribe to this worldview or whether to take a different perspective altogether. In trying to be a good father to my young son, I want him to be able to celebrate the things that he is good at. In that sense, I have chosen to abandon my mother's notion of "I" trouble. And that reminds me that I always had the choice so to do, although for most of the time, I have chosen to be constrained by that particular perspective that she held. But I cannot blame her for this, as I made that choice.

Of course, there are instances where human beings have been denied the chance to choose a contrary position in light of the aggressive power arrangements that they faced. But even there we have to concede that we have made the choice to comply in the face of those circumstances. Ultimately, we can choose whether or not to rebel – and that decision will be informed by our interpretation of where we find ourselves in the world and how we want to live our life in that context. Existing circumstances – best described perhaps as the status quo – are often experienced by us as something that urgently needs to be changed and, at the same time, that which feels the most beyond our capacity to change.

In light of this conundrum – a key point at which the ideas of transcendence and facticity intersect – a starting point for our examination of this might usefully be this:

> *As a free person, you can ask yourself …*
>
> What choice would I most like to make … and what stops me from making it? What small adjustments can I choose to make that might affect overall the situation that I face and that I am eager to change?
>
> *And, as someone who has positional power to impact on others around you, you might ask yourself …*
>
> What "ways of doing" and "ways of being" prevail in the workplace that might inhibit meaningful freedom there … and what can I do to remove them to create greater room for freedom?

Just to reinforce the importance of the freedom that we enjoy, it is worth restating that we create ourselves from nothingness. Across the course of our lives, we are negotiating a freedom that is absolute in terms of our existence … yet must be recognised as limited, in relation to the lives we live beyond the mere individual. This means that whilst we engage with the world as an individual, we need also to recognise the way in which our freedom might impact others. This makes our anxiety in respect to facing up to that freedom all the greater.

With that tension in mind, it is worth reminding ourselves that "My job is not my being … and my being is what matters to me, in terms of the time I have to spend in the world". I have talked extensively in the earlier chapters about how vital it is that we escape essentialism, by which I mean the idea of labels or identities that prevent us from existing in the moment.

We define ourselves – and should work to refuse being defined by others or by some notion of self that we then feel compelled to embrace.

Eschewing essentialism requires us to turn away from our "waiterness", to return to Sartre's example of a waiter being seen to be too "waitery" because they have opted to surrender themselves to the ideas behind that role instead of merely living in the moment and using their freedom there and then. The existentialist concept of freedom suggests usefully that while I may feel that some choices are denied to me it remains the case that I am free to choose how I *feel* about things.

In a corporate context, this contestation of essentialism can be used to flatten the workplace not simply in terms of some organisational design exercise but in respect to how we all relate to one another in it. This offers a useful starting point, which is as follows:

> *As someone referred to as a leader in a company setting, you need to constantly remind yourself that ...*
>
> I am free to lead, but do not want to indulge the idea that I am a "leader". To be a leader is to lead: the act precedes the title, in the same way as existence precedes essence.
>
> *And, as an individual, it is important to celebrate that ...*
>
> I am free to lead, despite not carrying the label of "leader". Leadership is a way of being and, off the back of that, of acting in the world. It is not a gift granted in terms of a title; it is the sum of our existential freedom and choices in the world, particularly in the workplace.

In the discussion on freedom, we heard a range of people describing their experiences in this regard and how they made their way through this complex terrain. We heard about how there was often a trade-off to be made in terms of acting in the world of work and the restraints that exist in that space, which means that those who are notionally in charge need to use their freedom to grant those around them a similar sense of freedom.

Others looked to emphasise the act of choosing choice – and recognising their agency in a wide range of settings. It was usefully stated that hierarchy can very often have a negative impact on people's confidence in terms of using their freedom – and that trust in this instance is absolutely essential. Lastly, people discussed the way in which business contexts wherein meaningful autonomy – as opposed to mere corporate lip service in regard to people's discretion to act – and the capacity to pursue one's own line, as opposed to following that of someone else further up the pyramidal structure, offer people insight into the freedom that they possess and provides them with room in which to make choices.

This was a take on existence in the workplace offered by just a few generous people who gave their time, their experience, and their thinking. Yet again, then, a reminder of the vital importance for those who find themselves choosing to manage or lead a workplace to recognise that freedom means making the choice to stop talking and leave the silence as an open space into which other – often subaltern – voices might step. *We need to take ownership of our freedom – and create space around us for others to possess their own freedom.* The corporate world is full of constraining definitions arising out of artefacts such as titles and expectations, corralling people into ways of being. Instead, we need business – and the people who direct it – to abandon these constructs and allow generous and honest space for people to be.

Chapter 3: Taking time

The simple fact that all of us have an end is something that we spend a lot of our time and effort keeping firmly out of mind. It is a crucial fact of life over which we exercise no choice (even if we're a plutocratic tech businessperson with too much money and an acute recognition in light of our circumstances that "There are no pockets in a shroud"!) This means that – instead of seeking constant distractions from this cruel certainty – we need to consider the finitude that we face and decide exactly how we want to spend our time.

Just because people all over the globe have been trained – and train themselves – to get up early in the morning; commute somewhere or shuffle over to their computer to stare at their faces on Zoom calls, do what they're told by those up above and direct people below them how to do their jobs, spend their weeks working for the weekend, does not necessarily mean that this is the way that we must spend our lives. It is a recognisable way of being because it has been around for a while – and most of us have found ourselves thrown into this setting and hence experience its familiarity as something that renders it unchallengeable.

Before continuing with this argument, I will pause here to offer a very personal observation that I am acutely aware in the five years since the world locked down and humankind realised the virtue of communication platforms such as Zoom and Teams as a way of keeping the world working, that these technologies are grim *memento mori* as well as sophisticated communicative means! Day by day since we began using these ways of connecting, I have daily glimpsed sight of images of myself slowly yet noticeably ageing as I sat on these calls. I know that some people turn off their image when engaged in this way, but my neurotic nature cavils at the idea of making myself disappear like that.

Back now to the structure of our working lives: there is a Camusian absurdity to be discerned in considering the way of being that most of us have ended up embracing … and this seems best expressed by a quotation attributed to the US journalist Ellen Goodman, which pointedly remarks that

> Normal is getting dressed in clothes that you buy for work and driving through traffic in a car that you are still paying for—in order to get to the job you need to pay for the clothes and the car, and the house you leave vacant all day so you can afford to live in it.
>
> (Goodman, 2008)

Camus's nihilism in the face of this absurdity denies the idea that it might be possible to make meaning out of such a ridiculous way of living. That is what – for me – makes existentialism better in terms of supporting people to work through the despair that the world can so often create within us. While nihilism invites us to face up to – and face down – the negativities that exist for us, it wilfully offers no means by which we might come to terms with this ridiculousness. Philosophically, then, existentialism offers us choice when confronting specific circumstances, whereas nihilism takes an absolutist line. In that regard, the former invites everyone to consider the following question:

> If there is no way in which to not live in this way, how best can I create a sense of purpose for myself in the face of this absurdity?
>
> And how can I support others around me to find meaning in the midst of this curious situation?

Notwithstanding how crazy Goodman's superb summary makes the world seem – again, in the spirit of Freud's notion of the uncanny, we are confronted by something that feels familiar but which, in terms of this framing, suddenly seems ridiculous – we are also faced by a consideration of how we choose to spend our finite amount of time. We find ourselves pastimes by which to pass the time and sometimes speak openly of finding ways to fill our time. Given the value of this limited resource, living a life in which we merely pass or fill our time seems to lack a vital level of thoughtfulness. This might prompt us to ask:

> How do we currently spend our time – and does that, on reflection, feel like a good use of that time?

> If we weren't passing time and filling time, what could we be doing with it instead?

When it comes to time in a corporate setting, there are two things to consider, one of which relates directly to this idea of passing and filling the time. We are all familiar with the practice of clock watching, counting down the minutes until the end of a period of contracted time in the workplace. As noted elsewhere in the book, when I was an operating department orderly all those years ago, I was expected to clock in at 8am and clock off at 5pm; you literally had to insert a card into a slot on a clock device, which would mark you in and then mark you out. In most workplaces, when confronted with a tedious meeting, of which there are a good many in organisational life, or working one's way through a grindingly dull task, we surreptitiously watch the time drizzling away.

In the course of the working week, we count down the days – forcing our way through Monday, clambering eagerly over hump day, and landing joyfully at late on Friday, when the 9-to-5 can stop and two days to ourselves, doing largely what we want, can begin. And, over the course of the seasons, we find ourselves cantering from one period of leave to another, looking forward to our high days and holidays and counting down the time until they arrive. We need to acknowledge this, rather than perpetuate the fairy tale that work is the be all and end all for everybody … and that acknowledgement should occur at an individual level – recognising that for some of us work is not our life and might actually be seen to be something that gets in the way of a meaningful existence – and in terms of creating a sensible working context where we concede that people will do their work to the best of their ability but that they are purely instrumental about it.

Lastly, we must face the fact that our experience of time in the workplace is grotesquely distorted by the decidedly corporate – and somewhat dehumanised – agenda in terms of getting things done. If you are a manager or a leader, you might choose to combine with others looking to fulfil the same or a similar role and openly commit to the following:

> I will actively cease *colonising* the future as my exclusive preserve and …
>
> I will stop referring to the past as if it were a *cemetery* full of past ideas, company failures, and forgotten personnel and finally …
>
> I will embrace my *presence in the present*, as the place wherein I can be in contact with myself and with others, the better to engage with life and make decisions about it.

If we accept the existentialist view that time is a deeply personal and precious resource, there is an urgent need for each and every one of us to take control of our time and use it as best we can and as we choose. In light of this, the organisations where we work – and the people who manage and lead – need to actively acknowledge that time belongs to all those who choose to come and work in their organisation. In consequence, they have a responsibility to loosen their control on time in general and the time of others in particular. A practical starting point for many in this situation would be to cede a level of autonomy to their people to work as, when, and where they can, allowing them to fit work around life rather than vice versa. This opens up the question for those in leadership positions:

> Do you have the personal strength and professional courage to surrender your control and stop trying to dictate where and how people do things?

Chapter 4: Making meaning

The workplace is far from being the blank canvas that much corporate ideology intimates that it is. For those involved in organisation development and similar practices, this means that it is essential that our activity begins with an immersion of ourselves in the complicated text of the company in which we are invited to work. A superficial scan of that text might well lead us to focus on the dominant narrative, the loud voice of the self-appointed narrator of the story. But following just that thread will lead us to assume erroneously that everyone is subscribing to the meaning that appears out of that text.

Instead, we need to seek out – under, behind, within, and alongside that dominant narrative – all of the stories that exist in that place. There is, of course, an extremely strong likelihood that each and every person who has cause to associate themselves with a given workplace will have a story to tell. As we see in Akira Kurosawa's fascinating film *Rashomon* (1950), even a single incident occurring in space and time and experienced by a number of separate yet connected individuals has the potential to be described differently by each and every person who witnessed it.

However, in one of our weekly conversations that took place on 14 March 2025, John Higgins and I ended up envisaging the myriad stories (or interpretations of a single event by a range of people) as a mosaic made up of a number of tiles. However, insofar as telling stories is something that is far from fixed (given that people's reflexion and understanding of the situation of which they are speaking will develop and possibly change over time), these mosaics are in a constant state of flux, so the patterns that come and go are kaleidoscopic rather than fixed. And we all of us need to be aware of this, as we insert ourselves in the text of the workplace.

The mosaic does not simply offer up a story board of different interpretations, one of which will be accorded a privileged position considering the seniority of those who tell it. Instead, it is a rich picture of the full range of meanings that people are deriving from their existence in the workplace, all sitting alongside one another. Importantly, given the over-interpretive nature of so much organisation development and senior leadership practice, the temptation will be to scientise the rich picture of multiple stories by clustering them and drawing themes out of that activity. Regrettably, this intervention ends up silencing the voices in that realm, in that it extracts meanings discerned by all in that context and clumsily conflates them with all the others, thereby reducing the number of narrators in favour of a domineering overview.

If you are a manager or leader in a company, your contribution to it should be that you:

> Invite people to tell their stories whilst reassuring them that you intend to listen to them rather than subtly edit them on the basis of your positional power.
>
> Support the tessellation of the story mosaic without succumbing to the temptation to impose your reading of the separate stories or an overview of that story collection.
>
> Recognise that the stories of existence in the workplace that people are finding their voice to tell can also be read as detailed descriptions of the meanings that people are deriving from their experience as a human agent in that context.

This will mean that there is an open and public acceptance of the unavoidable (but ordinarily suppressed) fact that there are multiple meanings in the workplace – and a wide range of motivations across the workforce. Because work itself can often be seen to be providing meaning for us as human agents, it is essential that we are aware of what that meaning is and how we experience it. This is the space into which we can all of us step to bracket off the corporate values and instead bring to the fore the values that bring us to work in a particular place at a particular time in our lives and to do the work that we are asked to do to the very best of our ability.

In the course of scrutinising the meaning and motivation we derive from work and the values that we associate with it, we may find that we are deriving nothing from this experience. This is despite the fact that it is likely to dominate five of the seven days in our week and may be managerially permitted to creep into the two days that are in theory set aside for our personal lives in contrast to the segments of our lives that we sell to another person in order to earn money to feed, clothe, and shelter ourselves and our families. This would, of course, be an existential prompt to rethink your situation and consider the range of choices that exist for you in this regard.

By driving our focus back into the heart of the organisation as opposed to privileging that which happens at the pinnacle, we will effectively be decentring the meaning that arises at the peak and dominates in light of the power with which it is imbued. This is a chance for us all to recast the corporate vision and mission as an imposition on everyone in that organisational space, whether we are on the frontline of the business or sitting in the boardroom.

Linked to this is a requirement for everyone toiling away in all of the shops, factories, and offices across the global economy to openly pronounce that "All the workplace is NOT a stage!" Ascribing to an essentialist view of the workplace, wherein we end up tucked into a role, label, or title, will distort the meaning that we look to derive from work, as that arises out of existing in a workspace rather than playing a role therein. A quick dismantling of the essentialist perspective might be achieved by addressing the following questions:

> What am I called at work and what is that title taken to mean in that specific context (and by whom)?
>
> What role is allocated to me, in terms of how what I am expected to do is defined in the particular place where I work?
>
> To what extent do I do my work in response to the title and role ascribed to me?
>
> How might I make choices that allow me to be me at work, as opposed to trying to be the me that others expect me to be?

Crucially, when it comes to title and role, it is the case that the essentialist versions of activities such as managing and leading need active challenge, for the sake of those trying to live up to those expectations and those who are then forced to endure that enactment of these lives. To turn up at work assuming that you are going to be a "manager" or a "leader" distracts the person seeking to "fill" these roles from the key business of managing and leading, which is turning up as a human agent and thoughtfully and ethically navigating all that confronts them in those circumstances.

Instead of declaring "I am a manager" or "I am a leader", actively embrace your humanity and the unknowability of the world in order to turn up in the space as an agent seeking a way through the existential challenges of the workplace. Some speak of leaving rank at the door, but – in so many corporate settings – rank is merely signified by an arbitrary descriptor. Instead, the challenge is to completely step away from rank in favour of a fulsome embrace of agency.

Lastly, in respect to the discussion of meaning, we have concentrated on individuals for most of the time. This is unsurprising in light of the focus of existentialism. However, it is very much my view that perhaps the most significant choice that an individual can make is to join with others as part of a collective. This is not to surrender oneself or to succumb to the pressures of others; it is about connecting with others as they seek to find their way through their lives and thereby using the power of individual change to create a movement for wider change. Critically, it sees a group that comes together voluntarily (wherein the various individuals keep their involvement in the collective under constant review) assume a position to create collective meaning. This is not an ideology to which everyone needs to subscribe, but a momentary shared experience and perspective to the benefit of all involved.

Chapter 5: Choosing choice

It has been acknowledged throughout this exposition that the linked notions of freedom and choice in existentialist thought require careful consideration and exploration. It is apparent throughout our lives that the freedom we enjoy – whilst absolute in a literal sense – and the choices that we then go on to make off the back of that intense personal liberty – is bounded by numerous expectations and limitations, which we inevitably find ourselves taking into consideration.

Recognising this bounding and restraint of our capacity to choose is perhaps the most important choice we can make in respect to our existence in the world. This is why I took time to carefully make it clear that the act of decision needs to be thought of as just one critical aspect of choosing. The inquiry and thought that precede that decision is where we carefully explore the nature of choice in our existence – and hence prepare ourselves mentally to be able to decide on the basis of careful reflection and appreciation of circumstances. In summary, then, choice goes beyond just decision; our active engagement with the world precedes on each occasion the decision that we then need to make.

It is also important to bear in mind that refusing to choose is a choice in itself. Alongside this sits the observation that there is no choice without sacrifice: in deciding on one pathway, I am obviously excluding all others, which carries a cost. As a vegetarian, there were in years past many instances in restaurants where I faced a soviet-style choice of what I could have to eat, insofar as there was just one starter and one main on the menu for someone with my dietary requirements. Increasingly, though, I am confronted by two or even three options. Unless I am feeling particularly hungry – or just plain greedy – choosing one dish denies me the chance in that moment to have the other dish/es.

Overall, then, we all need to be mindful of the importance of actively engaging with choice and decision, so it is useful to consider the following questions to explore how we are engaging existentially with this facet of human agency:

What are the choices that I have made in terms of my thinking about the practical choice with which I am faced?

How are the complex circumstances impacting my capacity to exercise my freedom and make a choice?

What constraints exist in respect to how I can think about the choice before me – and can I find ways to overcome them, can I find the capacity to simply ignore them, or will they limit the decision that I can actually make?

How is my choice likely to impact and influence others, for good or ill? Do I feel ethically content with this choice and its likely effect on me and others?

We are the product of our choices, so there is an urgent requirement if we opt to live in an existentialist fashion that we should give careful consideration to the circumstances we face and the decisions that we make in that context. This is something that we need to keep under constant review. And, in the workplace, if we are someone who looks to manage and lead in the organisation, this is all the more important, because of two things:

Our choices might not actually be choices in any meaningful sense, as we may simply be choosing to dance to the corporate tune;

The choices that we make are all the more likely to have a profound impact on other people at work.

Chapter 6: Being true to yourself

In existentialism, the human agent is the measure of all things, which is why living in an existentialist fashion demands that we attend properly to the issue of ethics. Existentialism is a way of philosophising, as opposed to a philosophy with its own programme. Hence, whilst religions and other bounded philosophies claim a core belief and sets of principles that offer moral guidance, existentialism is all about simply being in the world … so ethics in this instance derive from the recognition of the responsibility that we each of us have for our own existence.

This is why being true to oneself is so incredibly important for those who seek to live a life guided by existentialism: it is the actuality of our lives and the way in which we choose to live them that provides ethical guidance in this realm and which defines our personal ethics in that context. Additionally, it is the case that attending to oneself and living a life that foregrounds the act of existence requires us to constantly force ourselves to confront the realities of what it is to be a human being in the world, rather than allow ourselves to seek distraction from that reality. This is what existentialist writers are suggesting when they speak of living in good faith or authentically: we recognise where we are and how we need to approach our lives, thereby turning away from all manner of activities that we could pursue to hide ourselves from the actual business of living a life.

We noted earlier how obsessed corporate life has become with this notion of the "whole self" and the importance that it places on that being compelled to show up in the workplace. Once again, this is an essentialist conceit that presupposes that hiding behind our day-to-day – indeed, minute-by-minute – existence sits some definitive reality of the "whole self". Once again, it is worth restating that existence precedes essence, our lives define who we are: essence does not exist other than as unhelpful models imposed on people, as a means of looking to control those individuals.

It is our responsibility to actively challenge the notion of the segmentation of self. The conceit of the "whole self" is a foundational notion that intimates that there are myriad components of a human life. Unless you can pull together these elements – whatever they might be – you cannot declare the existence of a "whole self". But existentially the self is in a permanent state of creation as we each engage with the world, make meaning therein, exercise our freedom, and make choices that, in turn, actively contribute to the self behind that. The corporate notion of "whole self" is an ideological creation that articulates in outline the image of the ideal employee, something that cannot exist in reality but which is enforced on people at work through various managerial expectations.

In order to explore how to live our lives in good faith and in an authentic fashion, it is worth challenging ourselves with the following questions:

> To what extent am I focused on attaining a particular state, in contrast to creating a state for myself through mindful existence?

If I am pursuing a particular state, whose state is that … one that I imagined for myself or one that can be seen to be an imposition on me by others?

If you are aspiring to a state of your own creation, where do you feel this might be coming from, in terms of the facticity of your existence?

If the envisaged state is the product of others and not you, who are they, what are they trying to impose on you, and why do you feel they are doing this?

These reflections are useful in terms of assessing the extent to which we are authentically living our lives – or if we are instead aspiring to live a "model" life. The latter often feels to be contextual, in that we end up personally crafting an image of living well in a circumstance such as the workplace – or we have an image grafted onto us by others therein, particularly those who presume to manage and lead us. As should be apparent by now, these are essentialist notions, whereas an existentialist focus requires us to shape ourselves on the basis of the moment-by-moment choices that we make across the course of our lives.

These questions also serve to remind those who look to manage or lead in our organisation that any vision that they might harbour about something like the "ideal employee" or what a particular role at work should look like constrains other human beings. Moreover, in light of that focus on a model of living, those managers and leaders are effacing the potential creativity of those around them to embrace their agency and to live their lives existentially.

It is a major challenge to managers to embrace this notion because "manager" is an essentialist notion, one that is skewed these days in terms of a cluster of facets that include such notions as decisiveness, ability to work at pace, and directiveness. So managers themselves can be trapped in a model of what they should be at work, which denies them the capacity to be thoughtful and innovative in regard to that practice. And foremost is the idea that "manager" is defined by the possession and use of power in a company setting – when the future of management and leadership in corporate settings can be seen to be dependent on the active eschewal of that power.

Unfortunately, if you allow power to define you as a manager, you are not likely to feel motivated to turn away from a reliance on that in order to open up a space for people to enjoy a level of autonomy that allows them to acknowledge their own power in the world. Such a choice demands the ultimate act of authenticity; it is a decision made in good faith, rather than simply allowing the status quo to tick along in light of the way in which it benefits you, which is a deeply selfish and unethical choice.

In respect to this existentialist idea of authenticity, in contrast to the essentialist interpretation of it in the workplace, there is an imperative for us all to move beyond self-distraction in order to embrace positive action. In giving choices a swerve, we are – of course – making a choice, and in turn we are living in denial of the complicated challenge of living our life thrown into the world and experiencing a boundless liberty in terms of how we make our way through that. We can challenge this by reflecting on the following:

> Am I sheltering behind *ways of being* to avoid the actuality of *being*?
>
> Am I denying the reality of my existence by immersing myself in distractions?
>
> Thinking about Sartre's waiter trying too hard to be a waiter, thereby avoiding the challenge of being a person, to what extent am I finding ways to turn away from my responsibility to choose a life for myself?

There are serious implications in corporate life for the way in which particular ways of seeing the world and engaging with it are privileged. As was argued, there is science as a practice, as a meaningful method through which to understand key aspects of the world in which we live. However, alongside that we can discern scientism as an ideology, the unthinking application of that method to every element of our lives. In a business setting, this sees the foregrounding of quantitative approaches and the reduction of complex elements of the world – such as the dynamics that exist between multiple human agents coming together to impose categories and numeric aggregates.

This overbearing fascination with creating a particular version of "evidence", even in situations that do not lend themselves to it, prevents two things: firstly, it stops us from acknowledging and utilising key insights that derive from instances where the scientific method is entirely inappropriate; and, secondly, it denies us the chance to complement the quantitative material with insights derived from people focusing on their lives from a phenomenological standpoint.

As noted, this is a practice that entails attending to our presence alongside various phenomena – and how we experience that including how we end up feeling about it. Husserl's approach to this practice invites us to bracket off preconceptions – and to immerse ourselves in the moment. As we pay close attention to our experiences and our embodied presence in those specific circumstances, we are also generating "data", although it is different – but equal to, in terms of robustness and usefulness – the spreadsheets, tables, papers, and analyses that clutter our business lives. Indeed, phenomenology can be used to engage with all of that material in order to assess our experience of it, instead of merely taking it for granted and allowing it to unquestioningly structure our world and our lives within it.

A quick assessment in this regard would involve us:

> Querying whether the quantitative material that dominates our lives in the business world is the right way of trying to understand the situations in which we find ourselves.
>
> Stretching the data boundary beyond the quantitative so as include data sources that are not about metricising, codifying, and categorising but which instead are about the experiences of those around us and their personal descriptions of these circumstances.
>
> Moving away from a reliance on methods that concretise the world in order to allow ways of recognising and describing our presence in the world to be taken seriously.

Being aware of living your life

Hopefully, the exploration above of how we might engage with the five elements of existentialism on which I have focused – namely freedom, temporality, meaning, choice, and authenticity – will prove useful to you, should you choose to embrace some of those ideas. Overall, however, the crucial message of this work should be seen to be that first and foremost we are alive and have agency in the world. Our presence in the workplace is secondary to that, although our time spent in that context represents a considerable part of the finite time that we have overall to spend here in the world. If we take the fact of temporality seriously, something that we so often and unsurprisingly find ways to distract ourselves from, then we have a crucial decision to make:

> Am I content with spending a significant amount of my life in a workplace circumstance that does not feel worthy of having so much of my finitude dedicated to it?
>
> And, if I find that I am not, can I live my life in a way that releases me from the existing restraints to my existence?

The answer to these tightly connected questions might have a radical edge to it, in that we might choose to step away altogether from investing ourselves in a situation that on reflection carries too little reward to be justified. However, we may alternatively embrace the facticity of our lives and commit to exist with a greater level of awareness, the better to be able to make choices in our workplace that feel as though we are taking ownership of ourselves and adjusting our circumstances to make them more tolerable. In either case, the world is how it is, but that's not necessarily how it needs to always be: change begins at a personal level but can then be encouraged across a wider terrain as people come together collectively.

In contrast to the corporate nonsense around "transformation" as an imposable facet of organisational life and of people acting as "change managers", two views of the world which can be seen as essentialist formulations that have currency in the world of business primarily because they apparently make that space more manageable, it is important to think about the way in which change is an intrinsic part of being in the world. From an existentialist position, we have freedom in this setting, regardless of whether or not we opt to exercise it, and, as a result, we are faced as individuals with choices that, one way or another, have to be made.

In terms of working to live a better life and consequently creating a better world, it is worth considering our presence in the following way:

> As an individual, I engage with the world intellectually the better to understand it and create a clear sense for myself as to how I wish to live in it, rather than accepting a way of being in the world that is imposed on me by others.
>
> In taking responsibility for the myriad choices with which I am faced as a human agent, I am directly accountable for the changes that occur to and around me as I live my life authentically.
>
> Having made change in and around myself as a person in the world, I am thereafter conscious that these reflect shifts in me but also indicate nuanced adjustments across the whole of humankind.
>
> Lastly, I am then able to make the ultimate choice for an individual, which is deciding whether or not to become part of a collective, wherein I can work alongside others to have a dialogue about our respective experiences of the world – and what we might like to see being different in that context and how it might be possible to achieve that.

Life and work

Our lives are majorly absorbed by the demands of the world of work. I have sought throughout this book to question the appropriateness of this for human beings who – to paraphrase Satan's response to God's asking where he has been – have limited time to go to and fro on the Earth, and to walk up and down in this wonderful world (Job 1:7). Indeed, it is useful to remind ourselves of the powerful observation that:

> The meaning of being alive is just to be alive ... It is so plain and so obvious and so simple. And yet, everybody rushes around in a great panic as if it were necessary to achieve something beyond themselves. The funny thing is, they are not even quite sure what they need to achieve, but they are devilishly intent on achieving it.
>
> (Watts, 1998, pp. 3–4)

Alan Watts is beautifully stating a vital existential truth. Yet we are compelled by an economic truth, which is that we are forced to work in order to live. And, in far too many cases, that is a far from positive experience, so we condemn ourselves to live a chunk of our lives in a way that does not leave us feeling content, let alone happy. However, existentialism suggests that, as people thrown into the world with a limited time to enjoy our tenure, we have freedom and the responsibility to make choices, decisions that in turn have the potential to help us to live a better life, a life in which we are able to be completely honest with ourselves. Crucially, stepping into that way of seeing our existence means that we are potentially making meaning and a sense of purpose for ourselves, rather than living under the umbrella of an external meaning.

Interestingly, one author suggests that, in the work of the writer James Baldwin, we can discern circumstances where the racial inequality about which he wrote so powerfully in the book of essays entitled *Notes of a Native Son* is actually a symptom of 'the existential anxiety haunting modernity' (Rogers, 2025). It is further argued that, in terms of working to avoid the void at the heart of our being when we are refusing to live existentially, we hide within the essentialist qualities of society at large. Baldwin suggests that:

> From this void – ourselves – it is the function of society to protect us; but it is only this void, our unknown selves, demanding, forever, a new act of creation, which can save us – "from the evil that is in the world".
>
> (Baldwin, 2017, p. 20)

This means that we seek solace in society in all of its elements, as it allows us to avoid embracing the freedom that we are granted in our existence. The workplace is a prime example of how that works in practice for most of us. Hence, we may well feel safe and secure in the rigid structural and cultural construction of the workplace. This means that we distract ourselves from the fact that this rigidity limits our existence in myriad ways. So, if and when we choose to existentially engage with the world of work in order to find ways in which to actively live our lives, we have to face the fact that abandoning the rigour means that we will have to face the void at the heart of our being – and live in a way that manages the angst that flows from that by exercising our freedom and seeking out our own meaning.

As I said at the very start of this work, this is a book about business but not necessarily a business book. My intention has been to remind myself and those who have taken the time to read this volume that ultimately we have to think seriously about our place in the world and the nature of the world where we find ourselves because that is fundamental – and precedes any thoughts about organisations and how things get done in them.

A business book might well conclude with a model, a framework, or a checklist for people to work their way through to assess the nature of their workplace and supposedly identify ways of improving it. I will finish by merely expressing my sincere hope that my analysis and ideas feel that they might be helpful in terms of supporting you to perhaps think differently about your presence in the world and about the world that you would like to inhabit for the time you have in it. Those changes start with the individual, of course, but then depend on people making the crucial choice to join with others in open dialogue and respectful connection in order to create all the more impactful change to nudge us hopefully to a better world in which to exist.

The exaggerated classical liberalism of libertarianism speaks powerfully of freedom – but does so in an atomised context wherein individuals plough their own furrow without apparently even acknowledging the presence of others around them. Existentialism puts the individual at the heart of its philosophising but works to avoid fetishising that isolationist stance. In that sense, existentialism feels more closely aligned to anarchism than to libertarianism, not least because of a shared interest in respect to the intimate relationship between the individual and the social.

There is also a strong sense of both perspectives being extremely mindful of not wishing to fill the void with human constructions, particularly in a society where God has been declared dead. This led to a rush to replace God with various aspects of modernity, which existentialism and anarchism contested (Wahl, 2017). Additionally, it is suggested that they complement one another in respect to the following:

> The revolution is not merely a social revolution, but an internal one as well – "revolt against himself" – in order to shed oppressive ideologies,

> or in Nietzschean terms, to overcome certain weaknesses within the self that stultify expression and the affirmation of life.
>
> (Wahl, 2017, pp. 565–566)

These important political distinctions aside, the following extract comes from the work of an ardent libertarian – yet seems to go to the very heart of the challenge that we all face as we confront our own freedom and consider how best to actively embrace that in the workplace, so that we find ourselves meaningfully living our lives rather than enduring a wearisome working life.

> For most people, freedom remains a pleasant fantasy — something to dream of while carrying out daily obligations in the real world. They spend their lives talking vaguely of what they want in life, what they think they're missing, why they don't have it, and who it is that prevents them from being free. For most people, freedom is an "if only." "If only it hadn't been for my wife, I would have been a success." Or "If only it hadn't been for Roosevelt (or Nixon or whomever), the country would be free." The unfree person can never fully repress his urge for freedom — whether he considers his jailer to be his family, his job, society, or the government.
>
> (Browne, 2004, p. 2)

Ultimately, the world of work can very often be seen to be absurd, as Camus observes in respect to existence itself. We should not immerse ourselves in it without first considering whether this is how we want to spend our relatively brief time in it. Thereafter, we need to interrogate how we might live that life better. And those who have arbitrarily found themselves in charge of work, the workplace, and the people therein need to acknowledge their core responsibility in that respect is primarily human as opposed to unthinkingly corporate. Together, we need to recognise and work to support a way of being that allows freedom, choice, authenticity, and personal meaning to be derived by everyone in their lives, particularly in their working lives.

One contribution to this ambition is founded on a sensitive and thoughtful interrogation of three strands of thought in respect to organisational life, namely the classical approach that imagines the company as a machine; the human relations perspective that foregrounds effectiveness as flowing from involvement, and systems theory, which sees the abandonment of organisational charts in favour of the mapping of information flows (Kelly & Kelly, 1998). These authors offer an organisationally relevant synthesis of systems thinking and existentialism in respect to managing organisations, a key feature of which *inter alia* is argued to be that 'Personality is seen as an open system trading with its environment' (Kelly & Kelly, 1998, p. 42).

This looks to offer us all a starting point for exploring our place at work from an existentialist position. As individuals, it advises us to abandon the idea of a fixed and predetermined personality in favour of an open engagement with all that surrounds us, particularly in respect to our freedom, choice, and personal search for meaning. As managers or leaders, it is an instruction that we should avoid trying to constrain the open system through which those around us will be looking to develop.

Bibliography

Baldwin, J. (2017). *Notes of a Native Son*. London: Penguin Classics.

Browne, H. (2004). How I found freedom in an unfree world. Retrieved 2 April2025, from Mannwest: https://www.mannwest.com/wp-content/uploads/2018/07/How-I-Found-Freedom-in-an-Unfree-World.pdf

Goodman, E. (2008). *Ellen Goodman – Quotes – Quotable Quotes*. Retrieved 24 March 2025, from Goodreads: https://www.goodreads.com/quotes/106564-normal-is-getting-dressed-in-clothes-that-you-buy-for

Kelly, J., & Kelly, L. (1998). *An Existential*-Systems *Approach to Managing Organisations*. Westport, CT: Quorum Books.

Rogers, M. (2025, 27 March). *Existential Liberalism: James Baldwin and the Problem of Freedom*. Retrieved 28 March 2025, from Liberal Currents: https://www.liberalcurrents.com/existential-liberalism-james-baldwin-and-the-problem-of-freedom

Wahl, S. (2017). Anarchism and existentialism. In N. Jun, *Brill's Companion to Anarchism and Philosophy* (pp. 559–581). Leiden: Brill.

Watts, A. W. (1998). *The Culture of Counter Culture: The Edited Transcripts*. Boston: Charles E Tuttle Company.

Index

Note: *Italic* page numbers refer to figures.

For Product Safety Concerns and Information please contact our EU representative GPSR@taylorandfrancis.com Taylor & Francis Verlag GmbH, Kaufingerstraße 24, 80331 München, Germany